The British West Indies Regiment

The British West Indies Regiment

Race and Colour on the Western Front

Dominiek Dendooven

Pen & Sword
MILITARY

First published in Great Britain in 2023 by
Pen & Sword Military
An imprint of
Pen & Sword Books Ltd
Yorkshire – Philadelphia

Copyright © Dominiek Dendooven 2023

ISBN 978 1 39906 769 0

The right of Dominiek Dendooven to be identified as Author of this work has been asserted by him in accordance with the Copyright, Designs and Patents Act 1988.

A CIP catalogue record for this book is available from the British Library.

All rights reserved. No part of this book may be reproduced or transmitted in any form or by any means, electronic or mechanical including photocopying, recording or by any information storage and retrieval system, without permission from the Publisher in writing.

Typeset by Mac Style
Printed in the UK by CPI Group (UK) Ltd, Croydon, CR0 4YY.

Pen & Sword Books Limited incorporates the imprints of Atlas, Archaeology, Aviation, Discovery, Family History, Fiction, History, Maritime, Military, Military Classics, Politics, Select, Transport, True Crime, Air World, Frontline Publishing, Leo Cooper, Remember When, Seaforth Publishing, The Praetorian Press, Wharncliffe Local History, Wharncliffe Transport, Wharncliffe True Crime, White Owl and After the Battle.

For a complete list of Pen & Sword titles please contact

PEN & SWORD BOOKS LIMITED
47 Church Street, Barnsley, South Yorkshire, S70 2AS, England
E-mail: enquiries@pen-and-sword.co.uk
Website: www.pen-and-sword.co.uk

Or

PEN AND SWORD BOOKS
1950 Lawrence Rd, Havertown, PA 19083, USA
E-mail: Uspen-and-sword@casematepublishers.com
Website: www.penandswordbooks.com

For Madelon

Contents

Introduction		ix
Chapter 1	The British West Indies	1
Chapter 2	A British West Indies Regiment	12
Chapter 3	West Indians in France and Flanders	32
Chapter 4	A Troublesome Demobilization: Mutiny and Difficult Return	57
Chapter 5	Personal Trajectories	70
Chapter 6	West Indian Veterans between Nationalism and Pan-Africanism	83
Conclusion		91
Appendix 1: Composition and Service of the British West Indies Regiment		94
Appendix 2: Writing the History of the British West Indies Regiment		96
Acknowledgements		105
Bibliography		108
Notes		116
Index		122

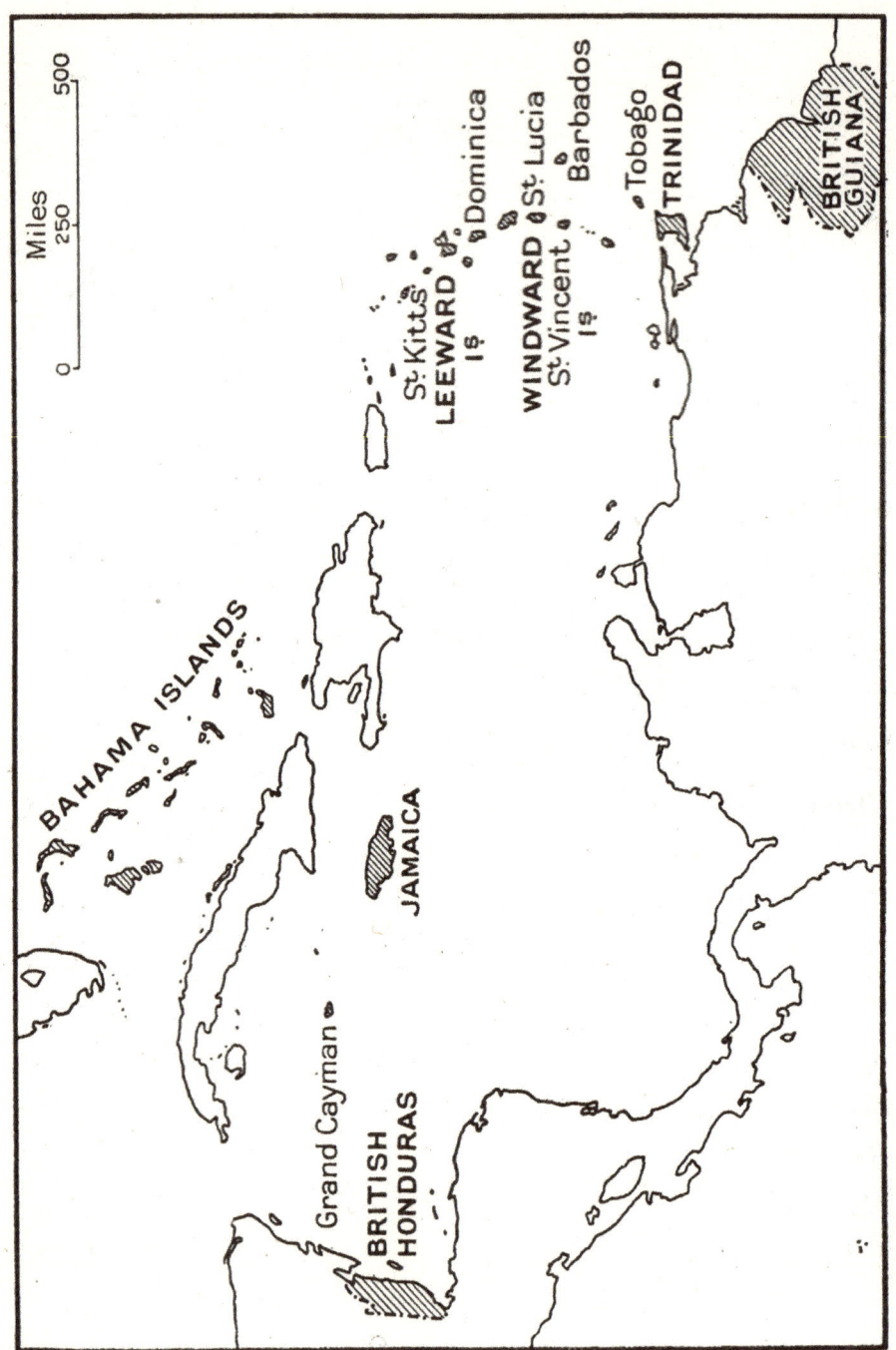

Map of the British West Indies, with distances, 1930.

Introduction

In September 1920 the great African American leader W.E.B. Du Bois asked why there was not 'a great British West Indian Federation, stretching from Bermuda to Honduras and Guiana and ranking with the free dominions? The answer was clear and concise – Color.'[1]

The issue of skin colour is indeed the thread running through this book: it defined social relations in the British West Indies, and it was the basis of the subordinate position of the British West Indies Regiment (BWIR) during the Great War. For if the men who made up its rank and file hadn't been 'black' or 'coloured' (i.e. 'brown'), it would have ranked on the same level with regular British (infantry) regiments. There might even never have existed a separate British West Indies Regiment as all men would easily have been integrated in regular British battalions. Yet, this was not the case and the only reason was because the men were, at least partly, of African descent.

And while one could argue that a separate treatment due to their skin colour was not unlike the attitudes in the British armies towards, for instance, the Māori in the New Zealand Expeditionary Force, the First Nations in the Canadian Expeditionary Force or the South African Native Labour Corps, there are some important differences between the servicemen from the West Indies and other non-white servicemen of the British Empire's armies of the First World War. Māori, First Nations, and Black South Africans were all *indigenous* groups in a predominantly white settler's society. All three were operating within the further context of the clearly defined separate polity of a dominion, respectively New Zealand, Canada, and the Union of South Africa. One of the consequences is that, unlike the West Indians, their post-war demands could only be focused on civil rights and more inclusion into the existing polity, and not on autonomy.

While maybe less 'exotic' than Zulus, Māori, or Sioux, the West Indies are a most interesting case if we want to lay bare imperial contradictions and expose attitudes of white superiority feelings that cannot be excused by paternalism à la 'the white man's burden'. For one, the African Caribbeans were not indigenous. While some territories, especially the mainland colonies of British Honduras and British Guiana, had a significant native Amerindian population of Maya or Caribs, in the overall picture of the British West Indies their numbers are negligible. The overwhelming majority of the black West Indians were just like their European fellow-countrymen equally descendants of settlers, though by force (brought over as enslaved people) rather than out of free will. And unlike the Māori and the Canadian First Nations, but not unlike the South African 'natives', they were not a quantitative minority in their lands but constituted the bulk of the population.

Secondly, the British West Indies were not a dominion, but a conglomerate of British colonies of different status in and around the Caribbean Sea. These territories had a large varying degree of autonomy and self-determination, going from none at all to considerable, though in the latter case it was always limited to the much smaller European component of its population. In the end, all colonies were much more directly governed by London than the dominions with their home rule. One of the consequences was that the allegiance of the population was always in the first place to London, Britain, and the Empire, and not to a semi-independent and increasingly self-conscious dominion. And there was not only the (political) loyalty to Britain: the West Indians genuinely felt

British, they identified with Britain and its Empire. English was in most cases their mother tongue and British was their culture and their education.

There are more characteristics which make the British West Indies Regiment a fascinating case worth an in-depth study. Its contingents were recruited, at least initially, from the (more) educated portions of the population, and included many who were self-conscious, reflected upon their situation and treatment, debated and agitated. Moreover, the regiment was established precisely because a significant number of 'coloured' and black West Indians demanded the possibility to enlist, and thus it was a manifestation of their self-consciousness as British subjects, their allegiance to King and Empire and of their Britishness. And last, but not least, the BWIR was initially formed and trained as an infantry regiment: the men of the first contingents were trained soldiers and in no way considered themselves as auxiliaries. Its subordinated role would only be attributed by others once they were overseas. The main, if not the only difference between the West Indian servicemen and their white British counterparts was ultimately the colour of their skin. Therefore, the terminology in this book is necessarily 'colour-oriented' and terms as black, white, 'coloured' and brown are used in addition to African Caribbean and European.

The British West Indies Regiment should in no way be confused with the West India Regiment, an all too often occurrence, even in recent literature. The West India Regiment was a Regular Army unit in existence since the eighteenth century that had mainly served in Africa and would do so again in the First World War. Its men, all professional soldiers, wore exotic uniforms not unlike that of the French *tirailleurs sénégalais* and they were generally considered of a lower social class than the volunteers of the BWIR. Moreover, the West India Regiment was nearly entirely composed of Jamaicans, as opposed to the BWIR which was more representative for the West Indies as a whole. While the BWIR was demobilized shortly after the war and disbanded in 1921, the West India Regiment dragged until it was disbanded in 1927, knowing a brief revival between 1958 and 1962 as the defence force of the short-lived West Indies Federation. This book only concerns the British West Indies Regiment, for the reasons enumerated above, and because this regiment has been present on the Western Front, which is my geographical focus.

While the West Indian case is extremely interesting in the context of race relations during the First World War, it is not the easiest choice. Though some of its territories were densely populated, the British West Indies were far from the largest and most populous portion of the Empire. Consequently, the British West Indies Regiment was with some 15,000 members not a large body, and personal records or witness accounts are scarce. This is somewhat compensated by the survival of a handful of battalion war diaries and by the fact we are rather well informed by the careers of some notable individuals who served with the regiment. The situation of the territories as a conglomerate of non-unified colonies equally impedes the interpretation of the West Indian war experience. Despite common characteristics, each colony had its specificities which make for a variation of contexts in which the men were recruited and to which they returned. Moreover, as compared to India, China, or the dominions, there is a relative unfamiliarity with the Caribbean origin, at least in Europe. Representatives from Caribbean countries and territories are generally totally absent from commemorative events, and this was even so during the centenary of the First World War. It is for instance striking that in contrast to India and China, in nearly twenty-five years I have not once witnessed the involvement of a single Caribbean state, overseas territory, organization or even individual, apart from descendants living in the UK, in a Last Post ceremony at Ypres. And yet, the First World War IS commemorated in the former British West Indies and IS acknowledged as being a watershed in the region's history.

As I make clear in the historiographical essay at the end of this book (Appendix 2), the British West Indies Regiment is yet another relatively understudied but emerging subject within First World War studies and what this book wants to add to the existing body of scholarly studies is a reassessment of the importance of the Western Front for the West Indian war experience. After all, this was the war theatre where the majority of the BWIR had been exposed to modern warfare. I investigate how the West Indian rank and file experienced the war, how the men were changed through this war experience and what effect this had on the West Indian societies to which they returned. To this end, I extensively use personal recollections of West Indians, even if these are few and short, complementing it with what little information there is that has been written by local inhabitants of the front region on their encounters with West Indians. I also took into account the few snippets from the battalion's official war diaries that might hint at how the men lived through these formidable events. This strong emphasis on individual experiences has equally led me to explore some individual biographies that demonstrate the agency of the returned West Indian servicemen.

This book consists of six chapters. In a first chapter it is necessary to give a brief sketch of what is understood by the British West Indies, the territories it comprised, and their main characteristics. For if there are two reasons for the relative lack of academic works on the West Indies and their involvement in the First World War, it is on the one hand the unfamiliarity most have with the region and on the other hand the variety of the colonies included. Besides the variations from one colony to another, it is important for any study of a unified military unit of the region to stress the factors they had in common, of which the issue of skin colour was arguably the most important.

The second chapter focuses on the British West Indies Regiment: how it came into being, who belonged to it, and how it was organized.

As the formal establishment of the regiment has been well treated in other publications, I will only deal with it in brief. Much more attention will be paid to the motivations for joining up and the sometimes mixed emotions the formation of a regiment for black and 'coloured' Caribbeans aroused in the West Indian territories, with the colour bar as the main factor of contestation. As a paternalist endeavour, the framework surrounding the regiment is of particular interest, including the officers' class, and the establishment of a West Indian Contingent Committee responsible for providing comforts and transport from the West Indies to the theatres of war. To conclude this chapter, I not only reflect upon the human contribution of the individual West Indian colonies to the BWIR but also have a more searching look at the casualty figures of the regiment. While the existing historiography has given relatively more attention to the Middle Eastern front as this was the only theatre where West Indians have been engaged in combat, deployment figures and casualty figures suggest Egypt and Palestine may have been of lesser importance to the West Indian war experience.

For indeed 'France and Flanders' was the main theatre of war where the BWIR saw action, and the third chapter examines the nature of the regiment's deployment in Western Europe. When having a more detailed look at the casualty figures on the Western Front, it is clear that the number of West Indians killed compared to those who succumbed to diseases is higher than has always been assumed as the men of the BWIR were frequently subjected to enemy shelling. Yet, the West Indians soldiery's self-image, their attitudes, and their presence near the frontline contrasted with their de facto subordinate position which included the assignment of labour duties, accommodation of lesser quality and the rude behaviour on the part of some officers. While the West Indians had the opportunity to engage with the local population, with prisoners of war, and with other allied servicemen, they were also subjected to discrimination such as temporary segregation or the disproportionate imposition of disciplinary measures.

Towards the end of the war, the battalions which were present on the Western Front were concentrated near the south Italian town of Taranto to await demobilization and transport home. The discriminatory treatment and measures worsened and the men's anger at these and other injustices they had suffered culminated in a mutiny. As the Taranto events, considered by many a defining moment in Caribbean political awareness, have received considerable attention from most other scholars, in this fourth chapter of the book, I limit myself to what I consider the most important aspects of that episode. The mutiny and the formation of a Caribbean League were an expression of the political radicalization of many West Indian servicemen. Other events such as the race riots in the UK and the USA further galvanized the African-Caribbean view on their British overlords and their own situation of subordination. This unrest was imported into the British West Indies by the ex-servicemen and throughout the summer and autumn of 1919 a whole series of disturbances took place.

Through their individual war experience, the West Indians were changed and many became activists. In order to demonstrate the enhanced awareness of an important part of the Caribbean veterans and the impact their individual lives ultimately had on the post-war development of the colonies, I present a number of personal trajectories: that of journalists Clennell Wickham (Barbados and Grenada) and Étienne Dupuch (the Bahamas); musician Sam Manning (Trinidad); labour leaders and politicians Captain Cipriani (Trinidad), Buz Butler (Grenada and Trinidad), and Norman Manley (Jamaica); and Pan-Africanist agitators Samuel Haynes (British Honduras) and Sergeant Grant (Jamaica).

Yet, as we will see in the sixth and final chapter, the experiences of the West Indian rank and file during the First World War also had an indirect impact and political influence which extended far beyond the individual lives of veterans, beyond the individual colonies, and even beyond the Caribbean. Island nationalism and the pursuit of West Indian unity, both enhanced by veterans and their overseas adventures, would ultimately lead to a short-lived Federation of the West Indies and the independence of most West Indian colonies. But the injustice meted out to the African Caribbean servicemen equally inspired black nationalist and Pan-African movements and leaders such as Marcus Garvey who had an appeal and were active throughout the African diaspora. It renders a lasting importance to the war experience of what ultimately was a tiny proportion of a tiny bit of the British Empire during the war.

Chapter One

The British West Indies

The British West Indies is a generic term for the British dependencies in the Caribbean which at the time of the First World War comprised the following colonies: Jamaica (with the Turks and Caicos Islands and the Cayman Islands); the Bahamas; Barbados; Trinidad and Tobago; the Windward Islands: Grenada, St Lucia, St Vincent and the Grenadines; the Leeward Islands comprising of the presidencies Antigua, St Kitts and Nevis and Anguilla, Montserrat, Dominica, and the Virgin Islands; British Guiana and British Honduras. All, apart from the last two, are islands.

Some were among the oldest British colonies. The total population in the British West Indian territories was, in 1914, less than 2 million. The more northerly colony of Bermuda was never considered part of the West Indies, had its own units during the First World War, and is consequently not considered in this book. On the other hand, I do include the Bahamas, even if the country was by many not considered part of the West Indies. Men from The Bahamas did, however, consider themselves West Indian and joined the British West Indies Regiment in important numbers. The British Caribbean islands and territories never belonged to one and the same polity, apart from the all too brief period of the West Indies Federation (1958–1962) to which the Bahamas and the continental colonies of British Honduras and British Guiana who all had had contingents in the BWIR, would not associate.

Considering the diversity of these colonies and the relative unfamiliarity of most contemporary readers with the Caribbean, it is not an unnecessary luxury to give a slightly more detailed overview of the West Indies' constituent parts as they stood at the time of the First World War.

Jamaica (capital: Kingston) was, with its 850,000 inhabitants, by far the largest British colony in the Caribbean Sea on the eve of the Great War. The island was dominated by the sugar plantation system, though by 1914 the export of fruit, especially bananas, equalled or surpassed the sugar industry. The elite was formed by the whites who accounted for just two per cent of the population, followed by a brown middle class who tended to identify themselves with the lighter skinned upper classes rather than with the bulk of the population. The majority – more than seventy-five per cent – was black and – save some notable exceptions – subsisted as tenant farmers and wage labourers. In the decades before the Great War, the literacy rate had increased considerably reaching sixty-two per cent by 1911. Yet, in the same period the agricultural workforce had been in steady decline while employment in industry and services remained static. The result was a net emigration of about 120,000: men who went to work on the Panama Canal, in the USA, in Cuba, or in Central America. The drive to migrate was reinforced by a series of natural disasters that struck the island: the 1907 Kingston earthquake which had claimed 1,200 lives, had been followed by heavy rains in 1909; a drought and a cyclone in 1912 and hurricanes were to hit in 1915, 1916 and 1917.

A key event in the recent history of Jamaica had been the Morant Bay Rebellion of 1865 when more than 400, mainly black peasant workers, had been brutally killed following a riot. In its wake the Jamaican House of Assembly abolished self-governance, becoming a directly ruled Crown Colony with a Legislature with a limited number of elected members, the others being appointed. Based on property and income, the franchise for this partly elected chamber was limited to less than ten per cent of the male population, the result being that the vast majority of those of African descent had no role to play in Jamaica's societal order. Maybe as detrimental to the black Jamaicans' advancement was the abolishment in 1911 of competitive examinations for positions in the civil service as this effectively blocked bright dark-skinned young men from entering the service.

The Jamaican drafts to the British West Indies Regiment included many men who were residing outside the island, mainly workmen from the United Fruit Company's Central American plantations and from the Canal Zone in Panama. Especially after the United States entered the war in April 1917, all difficulties impeding recruitment in the Canal Zone were lifted, and more than 2000 recruits were therefrom shipped to Jamaica between May and August 1917. That the opening of the Canal had reduced available employment opportunities would have been an extra stimulant to join up. Eventually, the Jamaicans recruited in Panama would form a majority in the 10th Battalion of the British West Indies Regiment, while they amounted to not less than thirteen per cent of all servicemen in the BWIR.

Today, both the Cayman Islands and the Turks and Caicos Islands remain British Overseas Territories, while Jamaica became independent in 1962.

The archipelago of **the Bahamas** (capital: Nassau), with a population of 56,000, had strong economical connections with nearby Florida, and was already then famous as a winter resort for American visitors. The colony's principal products were sponges and tropical fibre, unlike the other islands not industries that would benefit from the war. Equally unlike most of the other Caribbean colonies it had a fully elected House of Assembly and thus enjoyed greater political autonomy, something that was also reflected in its somewhat more liberal press. After war broke out, several hundred Bahamians joined the Royal Navy, and later white Bahamians joined in or through Canada or, after the USA's entry in the war, the American Army. As in the other colonies, the 'coloured' inhabitants could only join the contingents for the British West Indies Regiment. The Bahamas became an independent country in 1973.

Barbados (capital: Bridgetown) was densely settled with a population of some 175,000 in 1914. Of all Caribbean possessions, it had the longest connection and probably the strongest link with Britain, giving it the sobriquet 'Little England'. It was generally considered, along with Jamaica, among the more developed colonies in the region. Politically it had the same status as the Bahamas, with an elected House of Assembly. Yet, the enactments of the elected chamber became effective only when ratified by the largely nominated and thus unelected Legislative Council and it was chosen by a very restricted franchise based on property. Being mainly a sugar growing island it prospered during the war due to the great demand in sugar. It would eventually gain its independence in 1966, becoming a republic in 2021.

Trinidad and Tobago (capital: Port of Spain), just off the South American mainland, was the most industrialized and in 1914 the second largest of the British Caribbean colonies with a population of nearly 350,000. That population was also very mixed with a European element of mainly French and Spanish descent and one third of the community composed of (East) Indian indentured labourers, but Trinidad had also a Chinese community. With a variety of produce such as sugar, cocoa, asphalt, and oil it was also fairly prosperous, though as elsewhere in the region, the wealth was very unevenly distributed. Trinidad and Tobago had a Legislative Council with – in 1914 – only unelected members. During the war more than 450 islanders, mostly of European descent, enlisted in Canada or England on their own, including thirty-four who joined the French Army. The racial division in the colony was exemplified by its white and slightly 'coloured' Planters and Merchants Contingents which sent nearly 300 men overseas separately from the black West Indian Contingents. Independent in 1962, Trinidad and Tobago opted to become a republic in 1976.

The Windward Islands was a Federal Colony, actually a confederation of separate colonies with a common governor-in-chief, while each island retained its own institutions.

Grenada (capital: Saint George's) was the southernmost and smallest of the three Windward Islands and the residency of the governor-in-chief. With more than 66,000 inhabitants it was densely populated and was (and is until this day) known as the spice island of the Caribbean, being one of the largest nutmeg producers in the world. Grenada gained its independence in 1974.

St Vincent (capital: Kingstown) had some 46,000 inhabitants in 1914 and its main products were sea island cotton and arrowroot, a fibre mostly used in Belgian and Northern French lace production. The island seems to have suffered economically during the war due to the depression in trade, sinking to a point where it had to ask the Imperial government to bear the costs of conveying some of its contingents to England. As Saint Vincent and the Grenadines it would eventually become an independent country in 1979.

St Lucia (capital: Castries) was the northernmost and largest of the Windward Islands with, in 1915, a population of just under 50,000. As in St Vincent, the economy seemed to have suffered under the war to the extent that the civil administration had to undertake the provision of an adequate supply of food for the population. St Lucia gained its independence in 1979, being a member of both the Commonwealth and *La Francophonie*, the latter reflecting the fact that St Lucian creole French is the vernacular language on the island.

The **Leeward Islands** (capital: Saint John's), with a population of about 130,000 was a federal colony, consisting of five presidencies: Antigua; St Kitts and Nevis; Montserrat; Dominica; and the Virgin Islands. They all had nominated legislative councils, apart from the Virgin Islands, which had none.

Of all Caribbean islands, Antigua was considered second to Barbados in 'Britishness'. The island housed the governor and federal administration. Sugar was its staple product, with cotton in its dependent island Barbuda. As Antigua and Barbuda, it acquired full independence in 1981.

St Kitts, Nevis, and Anguilla: While St Kitts, then also known as St Christopher was a sugar producing island, the staple product of the other two was cotton. In 1983 St Kitts and Nevis became the then youngest independent state of the Americas while Anguilla has remained a British Overseas Territory until today.

Montserrat produced mainly sea island cotton and limes. It is still a British Overseas Territory.

Dominica was by far the largest of the Leeward islands. Situated between the French colonies of Guadeloupe and Martinique it was somewhat more isolated from the other British islands and always had a much stronger French inclined culture with a majority of the population speaking Creole French. Its main products were limes and cocoa. Dominica gained its independence in 1978 and became a republic, member-state of both the Commonwealth and *La Francophonie.*

The British Virgin Islands whose main product was cotton, is still currently a British Overseas Territory until this day.

British Guiana (capital: Georgetown) on the South American mainland had a population of some 300,000. Unlike the other British West Indian colonies, those of African descent were outnumbered by (East) Indian indentured labourers who formed about a third of the population. Most Europeans were of Portuguese stock, having emigrated from Madeira after the abolition of slavery. Among the inhabitants were also a few thousand indigenous Caribs and between 2,000 and 3,000 Chinese. Unlike most other British West Indian territories British Guiana was not a crown colony and had a peculiar political system with chosen representatives in both executive and legislative bodies, something it had inherited from the time it was composed of several Dutch colonies. However, as elsewhere, limited franchise made these representatives the spokesmen for landlord elitism and conservatism.

Sugar and derived products were the main commodities produced in Guiana. A large number of those from British Guiana who volunteered for the British West Indies Regiment, more than 1700, have been refused on medical grounds, mostly as suffering from filariasis, a tropical parasitic disease transmitted biting insects that affects the lymph nodes and lymph vessels. As Guyana it became independent in 1966 and pronounced itself a republic within the Commonwealth four years later.

Small and poor, **British Honduras** (capital: Belize City), on the Central American east coast had a population of just over 40,000 of whom only 2,000 were of European descent. There were large Amerindian (Maya) groups, but the bulk of the population was of mixed descent (Mestizo, Kriol, or Garifuna). The origin of the colony lay in woodcutting and that was still the principal economic activity on the eve of the Great War. It was pretty much a frontier territory with no all-weather roads and a heavily disputed border with Guatemala. As Belize it gained its independence in 1981.

From this short overview it might be clear how different each of the West Indian colonies was. Far from being a homogenous entity, each colony had its particular social and political culture. While The Bahamas and Barbados had elected legislative assemblies and British Guiana an antiquated political system with elected officers, all the other territories were governed as crown colonies with limited or no elected members in their legislatures. A crown colony was ruled by governors appointed by the Colonial Office in London, who might be advised by officials but ultimately retained responsibility for the administration. The potential benefit of such rule was its amenability to British metropolitan opinions who were usually more enlightened than those of the local white elites. Yet, it was necessarily paternalistic and authoritarian.

The Bahamian Newspaper editor, politician, and First World War veteran Sir Étienne Dupuch explained that while all 'coloured' people came largely from the same area in Africa, the environments they had to live in had made them what they are. Hence, Jamaica, with its plantation economy, had what he called 'the roughest population', while the inhabitants of the Bahamas, where slaves had mostly been domestic servants, gained, according to Bahamian Dupuch, 'the reputation of being the gentlest folk in the Caribbean'.[1] Whatever the truth of such statements, the inhabitants of the West Indies clearly identified with their island home in the first place and only in second place with the West Indies as an umbrella term. Not only in the mind, but also in daily life, some of the territories were cut off from one another: there were no links between British Honduras and Antigua, Grenada, or Tobago, or even between islands within sight of each other such as St Vincent and St Lucia. A letter sent from Jamaica to Barbados went via Halifax, New York or even London. It is important to stress the geographical distances and the lack of regular inter-island shipping routes in 1914 as this obviously affected inter-island mobility and exchange in a negative way.

Yet, there were certain characteristics they shared. There was the importance of the sugar industry which in the 1920s employed about a tenth of the population in the West Indies. Most workers were black and ruthlessly exploited. Everywhere the role of the majority of the people was restricted to paying taxes and performing heavy labour. Trade unions were forbidden, the pay was low, and the long shadow of slavery meant that most white employers looked down on their 'coloured' employees. The slave past played a hugely important role in all of them and partly explains the general reverence for the monarch who was seen as the higher authority who could limit the powers of colonial officialdom and plantocracy. Britain was seen as the emancipator of slaves and the guarantor of freedom. Among the majority of the population in the West Indies, there was a genuine belief in abstract British ideals such as freedom, equality before the law, and respect for property which was only at first sight contradictory to the subordinate position they were subjected to in their colony: the ideas that were considered to embody the Empire were detached from the behaviour of the Empire's representatives and colonial elite.

And most inhabitants felt genuinely British. In the words of Glenford Howe: 'Centuries of alienation, indoctrination, creolization, and suppression of the remnants of African cultural practices had by the outbreak of war, created staunchly loyal black Britishers in the colonies'.[2] Jackie Turpin, whose father Lionel was a merchant seaman from British Guiana expressed it thus: 'He was descended from slaves taken from West Africa but English was his first language. His schoolbooks were written by British people; he lived under British law; he was brought up to admire British poets and British musicians and British scientists and British politicians and British nobility. His allegiance was to King George V, to his Mother Country and to British people all over the world.'[3] Throughout the British West Indies, the institutions, the education, the road patterns, the architecture, the sporting activities or the names of towns, streets and families, everything was British. Everywhere the mother tongue was English, apart from Dominica and Saint-Lucia where the local variety of Creole was and is the common language, yet English the official language. This means that, unlike in the motherland with its large Welsh- and Gaelic-speaking communities, there was no language issue and the culture high and low was mainly British influenced. And, apart from tiny communities such as recently immigrated (East) Indians, all were Christians.

So 'Otherness' in the British Caribbean territories was mainly, if not solely, based on skin colour. And ultimately it was skin colour that determined the role one was allowed to play in society. The general rule in this 'pigmentocracy' was: the more white, the more rights. There was an elite of colonial British and of white Creoles. The latter, born and bred in the colony, were closer to the 'coloured' bulk of the population with whom they had been at school. But being white they had privileges denied to the vast majority of the inhabitants. Despite the existence of a growing black and 'coloured' educated middle class, where often subtle and highly subjective social distinctions as to the whiteness of one's skin were at play, all people of (partly) African descent nowhere enjoyed the same rights as their fellow-countrymen of pure European descent. 'From the start we fell into separate groups, masters and slaves, rulers and ruled, white and black. With the milk of our black and brown mothers we absorbed the doctrine that white was virtue, power, and wisdom and that black was vice, weakness, stupidity', as the Jamaican historian Sir Philip Sherlock eloquently stated.[4] The colour bar was more of a fence, impossible for anyone to surmount who was not of the right complexion. C.L.R. James was clearly angry when he wrote around 1930 that '[The white men] keep on repeating that the negro lacks this and that and the other thing, and when they do give him a chance give him grudgingly and stand aside looking critically on waiting to jeer at his mistakes'.[5] According to the Norwegian anthropologist Eriksen it was precisely this virtual identical treatment as slaves and as underpaid and discriminated working class that enhanced the development of a distinctive 'black' ethnic category in the Caribbean (and the USA). Deriving from a collective stigmatisation based on colour rather than on place of origin or ancestral language, this shared experience would create shared political interests.[6]

While white superiority was taken for granted, it did not go unchallenged. In the decade and a half before the First World War, the British possessions in the Caribbean had seen a fair share of unrest: riots in Port of Spain (Trinidad) and Montego Bay (Jamaica) in 1902; resistance against the proposed union of Grenada and St Vincent and a riot in Georgetown (British Guiana) in 1905; riots in St Lucia and again in Port of Spain (with 14 killed) in 1908; and in Kingston

(Jamaica) in 1912. While many of these had been labour protests in the first place, they inevitably opposed black against white, due to the large extent in which class distinction and colour distinction coincided. This phenomenon of riots would continue after the Great War. To the white population, the riots of the early 20th century were a reminder that arming a part of the black population or allowing them to gain battle experience could threaten the colonial status-quo. It explains the reluctance by many whites in the West Indian colonies to see their black fellow-countrymen going off to war.

Chapter Two

A British West Indies Regiment

On the outbreak of war in 1914, there was a general upsurge of patriotism in the West Indies. Many black men offered to enlist. This they were fully entitled to do: the Manual of Military Law précised that 'any negro or person of colour, although an alien, may voluntarily enlist'.[1] He would then be qualified as any other British subject, but could not be promoted to a commissioned rank, a rule that would be maintained until 1939. Yet, the recruitment of 'coloured' subjects was something of a dilemma to the Colonial Office: while it wanted to encourage the West Indians to enlist, it also supported the view of the War Office that in any case black West Indians should not be used against white forces. The prevailing establishment view was perhaps best expressed by Lord Dundonald, a major landowner in the West Indies, when he wrote to the Secretary of State for the Colonies, Lord Harcourt, on 23 November 1914 that he had been informed that lighter 'coloured' volunteers had been accepted but that black volunteers had been rejected. Though against the introduction of blacks into British regiments, Dundonald pointed out that failing to make use of the black population of the West Indies could potentially be harmful to the Empire as they might be tempted to swing to American support. Hence, he proposed a West Indian contingent for Egypt. Harcourt duly pleaded this proposal with the War Office, acknowledging that it would be 'impracticable' for a non-white West Indian contingent to serve in France 'for a number of reasons'. The only reason his note mentioned though, was skin colour. The War Office initially turned the Colonial Secretary's proposal down.² In the end it was a personal intervention of George V in April 1915 that would allow the formation of West Indian 'coloured' contingents for the war. After being urged so by the King, the War Office had to give in and one month later the formation of non-white West Indian contingents was approved. In October 1915 the British West Indies Regiment would be established, and recruitment could begin in earnest.

As with other subordinate groups the reasons to volunteer for the army in the British West Indies were varied and seldom univocal. In the 1999 TV documentary Mutiny, 101-year-old Gershom Browne (8 August 1898 – 6 December 2000) from Guyana who had served in the 1st Battalion invoked a sense of longing for adventure, stating that as a boy he read many war stories, while both 96-year-old Barbara Wickham of Barbados, whose veteran brother Clennell (21 September 1895 – 6 October 1938) later became a well-known radical journalist, and 106-year-old Eugent Clarke (1894 – 17 February 2002) from Jamaica who had served in the 4th Battalion, elicited mainly economic reasons. In the words of Clarke: 'It wasn't easy to find work in Jamaica and the pay was nothing'.³ The completion of the Panama Canal that had heavily drawn on Caribbean labour, mainly from Jamaica and Barbados, had closed one escape route for the unemployed, but the war now offered a new one. Christine Du Bois reckoned the remittances the BWIR men received indeed lessened economic hardship in the Caribbean and enabled some families to buy means to obtain a sustainable living such as fishing boats or land.⁴

When Eugent Clarke signed up, he left home in civvies but returned in uniform. Upon his aunt's reproach that he would only be 'a German bait', Eugent answered: 'Never mind, I have to go for England. I like the old England'.⁵ There was indeed often a profound sense of patriotism involved. Black West Indians had been taught that it was Britain that had emancipated the slaves and that it was under Queen Victoria's reign that the system of apprenticeship that had tied their forefathers to their former master's estates had been abolished.

Overall, in the British West Indies there were genuine feelings of affection towards the Royal family who had freed their ancestors. Britain's past as abolisher of the slave trade was successfully invoked in the press and at war rallies: at one meeting the potential recruits were asked whether they were going 'to sit down and be slaves' or join up and fight like men.[6] That it was the same nation that had earlier lead the slave trade and had enslaved their forefathers was obviously not mentioned. Moreover, British rule was depicted as benign compared to German colonial policy which was considered opposed to 'the enlightenment of blacks'. According to Marcus Garvey (Saint Ann's Bay, Jamaica, 17 August 1887–London, 10 June 1940), the duty of those interested in the progress of the 'Negro' was to do all within their powers to stop German militarism.[7] Garvey had on the outset of war founded the Universal Negro Improvement Association (UNIA), a Pan-African organization he would take to great heights in the early 1920s, particularly in Harlem. He is considered one of the founding fathers of Black nationalism and Pan-Africanism, and there is a considerable historiographical production on Garvey and Garveyism. Considered a Jamaican National Hero, there is a Garvey statue and shrine in Kingston's National Heroes Park.

When in 1914 the *tirailleurs algériens*, *tirailleurs sénégalais* and the Indian troops arrived on the Western Front, their deployment was widely and favourably reported in the West Indian press. It reinforced the idea of a global and interracial rally in support of the Empire and its allies in which the 'coloured' men of the West Indies had to play a role. Richard Smith also points to a more subtle influence these reports could have had: though a negligible two per cent of the Jamaican population were Indian indentured labour, the Indians were often relegated to jobs that traditionally would have been considered women's work and this might have urged some black Jamaicans to fulfil the manly duty to go off to war.[8]

There certainly was more to it than patriotism: a hope that in return for loyalty unto death, these colonial subjects would be justly rewarded after the war, was equally a sentiment voiced by Marcus Garvey in his often-quoted telegram to the Colonial Office of 16 September 1914. In this telegram on behalf of the UNIA, Garvey had expressed feelings of support and loyalty 'mindful of the great protecting and civilizing influence of the English nation and people… and their justice to all men, and especially to their Negro subjects'.[9] He hoped that fighting on the battlefield would bring equality and political power. Garvey was not yet the influential figure he would later become, but his sentiment was shared by many others, including well-read local newspapers.

The *Federalist and Grenada People*, one of the main newspapers on that island, was outspoken on this subject. On 19 June 1915 its editor William Galwey Donovan had praised Barbados for sending a contingent to the front, so 'she may take rank with Canada and Australia and New Zealand and South Africa and Newfoundland', not coincidentally enumerating the five (white) dominions with home rule. He launched a call to arms towards the 'lesser islands', at the same time expressing his concern that there 'may be one obstacle to this. The skin and color prejudice, which dominate the minds of the English authorities'. Yet, he was convinced that 'This war, however, will end that.' Some months later, on 27 October 1915, when the West Indian contingents were being trained in England before being divided into several battalions and the population in the Caribbean believed the men would be allowed to prove their worth by fighting, the newspaper again gave voice to both its mix of loyalty to and criticism on the Empire and its conviction that a shared war experience would improve race relations:

> We will be fighting for something more, something inestimable to ourselves. We will be fighting to prove Great Britain that we are not so vastly inferior to the whites that we should not put on a level, at least, of political equality with them. We will be fighting to prove that the distinction between God-made creatures of one Empire because of skin, color or complexional difference should

no longer exist, and that the same opportunities should be offered the Colored subjects of the Empire as fall by right of race to its white citizens. We will be fighting to prove that we are no longer merely subjects, but citizens – citizens of a world Empire whose watchword should be Liberty, Equality and Brotherhood.[10]

The West Indians were not only going to fight against something, i.e. the enemies of the Empire, but also for something, namely to become citizens, i.e. men who take actively part in society's organization and who, regardless of their skin colour, have a say in their future.

The war was certainly seen as an opportunity for those advocating a West Indian federation: a common regiment was a first step towards the desired unity of the British West Indies, so argued T.A. Marryshow, the publisher of Grenada's other newspaper *The West Indian*. The ultimate aim would, also according to him, be a West Indian Dominion. Others reasoned that a visit to England and a closer association with British ideals would make the men even prouder to be part of the Empire.

Not all non-white Caribbeans, however, approved to support the war. While the exclamation of Eugent Clarke's aunt as him being 'only a German bait' could easily have been uttered by a European mother or girlfriend, Gershom Browne remembered some saying to him in British Guiana that it was 'a white people's war', which implicitly meant that blacks had nothing to do with it. Similar attitudes were recorded in Trinidad, Grenada, British Honduras, and Jamaica. In the northern districts of British Honduras, where many were of Mexican descent, young men fled across the Mexican border or into the jungle when it was rumoured they would be obliged to join up, and from some large villages not even a single man volunteered. Everywhere, the resistance against recruitment increased in the course of the war. In more than one instance, scuffles broke out between the recruits and police or bystanders, in particular in Trinidad and Jamaica where the bored volunteers often had to wait a long time for transport to Europe. While disturbances caused by mostly young misbehaving recruits was certainly detrimental for the recruitment drive, perhaps more worrying for the authorities was that the volunteers were sometimes jeered and insulted by members of the public. In Kingston in January 1917, men from the 5th Jamaican War Contingent were ridiculed by civilians who were encouraged by the police, after which the recruits retaliated, smashing shop windows, and attacking bystanders. It was the relative affluence of the contingent men, among them landowners from the country, that provoked resentment, in particular when they drew the attention of the townswomen.

The British recruitment officers were indeed selective and largely preferred the educated and generally lighter skinned working and middle classes to the 'undersized, ragged, barefooted set of fellows, who came forward probably to get a meal', as the commander of the local forces in Jamaica stated.[11] On that island not less than sixty per cent of the volunteers who came forward were rejected. In British Guiana it was even seventy per cent. Most of the men who volunteered and were accepted had at least enjoyed some form of education and being able to read and write in English was a prerequisite, as it – at least officially – was also the case in the United Kingdom. Illiteracy was even the highest known non-medical cause of rejection in the West Indies. Only in November 1916, after the heavy losses on the Western Front, was this requisition relaxed and men unable to read and write in English were henceforth accepted, something that might have had an impact in the territories where large segments of the population did not have English as their mother tongue, such as Saint Lucia, Dominica, or British Honduras.

While literacy was a requirement, being underaged was apparently less of an issue, even if 143 West Indians were registered as rejected because of being too young. Though as elsewhere in the British

Empire the age for volunteers was 18, quite a number of the recruits we encounter seem to have been of quite a tender age. Jamaican Herbert Morris was 17 when he was executed in Poperinghe in 1917 and he wasn't the only West Indian soldier of that age to die. Étienne Dupuch wrote how he was a 17-year-old orphan and considered himself still a child when he went overseas with the BWIR: while in France he was on more than one occasion addressed as *'petit garçon'*.

Early in 1917 Jamaica introduced a Military Service Act that required the registration for enlistment of men between 16 and 45, and by doing so it was the second colony of the British empire, after New Zealand, to accept the principle of universal military service. Similar conscription legislation followed in British Honduras and Grenada. Other colonies, including Barbados or Trinidad and Tobago, found it an unnecessary measure. Despite the acts, however, nowhere in the British Caribbean territories was conscription implemented during the Great War. As a consequence, all West Indians who served were volunteers. It is by no means incidental that the war diary of the 6th Battalion of the British West Indies Regiment starts explicitly with the sentence: 'This unit was raised by voluntary recruiting in the colony of Jamaica between November 1916 and March 1917.' These were indeed free men who had freely joined. And as Rev Alfred Egbert Horner, the chaplain of the 9th Battalion confirmed, they were very much aware of that: 'He is always conscious of the fact that he is a free soldier, no conscript and no mere labourer'.[12]

An interesting footnote in this respect were the attempts to convince the Caribs and Maroons to volunteer. Considered by the local authorities as a 'martial race', the indigenous Caribs (Kalina people) in British Honduras were reminded of their tradition of armed resistance against the British. Similarly, the Maroons in Jamaica had been successful in their struggle against the British. As descendants of African slaves who had escaped and had established free communities in the mountainous interior of the island, they were (and still are) held in awe by the Jamaicans. When the rumour spread that the Maroons would come down to join up, large crowds gathered to witness the event. But the Maroons never came. As with the Caribs, not only wide-spread illiteracy but more importantly cultural differences made the attempt to recruit them a failure.

Among the white components of the West Indian societies, public opinion was equally divided regarding the opportunity of African Caribbeans to join the army. While some white elite spokesmen, such as Herbert de Lisser in his conservative Jamaican newspaper *The Gleaner,* argued that the black West Indians would learn the value of discipline, self-restraint and obedience and hence would be easier controlled, many other European West Indians considered the recruitment of the 'coloured' portion of the population absurd and dangerous. Slave revolts and riots had been an integral part of the region's history, and oral tradition about these dreadful events had kept the fear of disturbances alive. Moreover, little had changed socially since the abolition of slavery, while the number of white inhabitants, already a minority, had been steadily decreasing in the recent past. Hence, the thought of more trained and armed black inhabitants, and the possibility of African Caribbeans helping to kill whites, even if they were enemies, was a source of anxiety among sections of the white population. Another concern, particularly in British Honduras and Jamaica, was the probable loss of labour. It was no wonder that the recruitment drives often encountered opposition from those who made up the local authorities. When Arthur Cipriani, later to join as captain, convened the first public recruiting rally in Port of Spain, no government official took any part in it. Yet, in order to keep a patriotic face, such objections were rarely openly voiced.

In the Caribbean the colour bar was so rigid that most white men could simply not imagine serving alongside black men (unless as officers): in Trinidad the white population formed its own Merchants' and Planters' Contingent and in Barbados a Citizens' Contingent was raised whose men were eventually integrated in British metropolitan regiments. The very name Citizens' Contingent is telling: these men considered themselves to be citizens of the Empire as opposed to the other Barbadians who were merely imperial subjects. Trinidadian C.L.R. James was seventeen and still a schoolboy when in 1918, he tried to join the Merchants' Contingent. Though dark skinned, he thought that as a tall and very fit man who was making a name as a cricketer, he stood a chance. It was not to be: 'Young man after young man went in, and I was not obviously inferior to any of them in anything. The merchant talked to each, asked for references, and arranged for further examination as the case might be. When my turn came, I walked to his desk. He took one look at me, saw my dark skin and shaking his head vigorously, motioned me violently away.'[13] In Trinidad and Barbados, the co-existence of a white contingent and a black contingent left many 'coloured' men stranded, namely those who didn't want to be associated with the darkest portion of society but who were at the same time considered too dark for acceptance in the white contingent. An attempt in Barbados to create a special contingent for this category did not bear fruit. It is, however, a clear reminder of how skin colour was the ultimate criterion for identification and self-identification in the West Indies.

Likewise, within the British military establishment there was a discrete policy to discourage non-white volunteers. Major General Sir Charles Edward Caldwell, Director of Military Operations and Intelligence at the War Office abhorred the idea of 'coloured' men handling hand-grenades: '...in the hands of such Natives they would be a greater source of danger to their friends than the enemy'.[14]

And even in the letter with which King George V conveyed his wish to allow the establishment of a British West Indies Regiment, it was explicitly stated: 'They might be usefully employed in Egypt', suggesting even on the King's behalf a reluctance to deploy non-white recruits in Europe.[15] This is eventually also what would happen: the first battalions of the BWIR were initially sent to Egypt. There it was decided that though BWIR battalions were to be transferred to the Western Front, the men would not be allowed to fight in Europe. The military trained West Indian soldiers would be employed to carry munitions to the guns, while further recruited contingents would be from the outset designated as labour battalions. In fact, only one of the West Indian battalions who remained in Egypt and the Middle East would – briefly – gain some fighting experience against the Ottoman armies in Palestine. The Turks were after all not considered really white in the eyes of the British military establishment and hence the West Indian deployment in Palestine could not be considered derogatory for the image of white supremacy. The British military establishment's attitude gives an interesting twist to the words of the soldiers' song recalled by Jamaican veteran Eugent Clarke in 1999:

> Goodbye, goodbye Jamaica.
> We're going to fight for our King and Country.
> We want to catch the Kaiser if we get the chance.
> If we get the chance.[16]

As if the Jamaican soldiers instinctively felt what was in store, they stressed the words 'If we get the chance'.

Though dramatic torpedoing or sinking did not occur in the West Indian case, troop transports from the Caribbean to Europe and beyond had its good share of tragedy. Eugent Clarke was in the third contingent from Jamaica on the infamous *Verdala*, a ship that got caught in blizzards in the Northern Atlantic. The vessel was unheated, and the men were only clad in tropical uniforms. The warm winter clothes on board were only issued when it was too late. Upon arrival in Halifax practically the whole battalion was frostbitten. Some men had to be amputated, two hundred others were sent to Bermuda to convalesce and at least nine died: Seven BWIR men have been buried in Bermuda, all died in April 1916. Two more died in Halifax. 'When we got to Bermuda, I was just creeping. I couldn't walk, just creep on my knees' remembered Clarke.[17] At last, he did make it to the front, after having returned to Jamaica to board a next transport. Obviously, what happened to the men on the *Verdala* did not have a positive effect on the recruitment campaign in Jamaica. But even without blizzards, transport to Europe proved to be agonizing. Étienne Dupuch's Bahamian contingent first had to travel to Jamaica whence it later continued to Alexandria. On board there was a doctor but no medical provisions such as medicines or a sick ward. He compared the hold of the ship to 'a scene in Dante's vision of hell.... the place was crawling with body lice left behind by previous troops transported on this ship'. Every day there was a funeral, usually of someone who had gone down with pneumonia. Yet, it was also here, in the hold of that ship, that he really got to know the men from the Out Islands of The Bahamas, people he would otherwise not have met and whom he called 'the hardened men steeped in evil practices'.[18]

The first West Indian contingent to arrive in Europe did so in October 1915 and was sent for training in Seaford on the English south coast, midway between Eastbourne and Brighton. As the recruitment in Jamaica was still in full swing, all men came from other parts of the British West Indies. A first battalion was formed with four companies, reflecting their origin: A Company – British Guiana, B Company – Trinidad, C Company – Trinidad & St Vincent and D Company – Grenada & Barbados. The first Jamaican contingent sailed for England on 9 November 1915, an event hailed by the island's press as Jamaica's arrival on the world stage.

The officers were not always of the highest quality, and this was one of the reasons why C.L.R. James considered the first battalions handicapped from the start: 'Officers of the old West India Regiment who were known to have been recruited from the Sandhurst failures were drafted to the BWIR, and old Colonel Barchard, appointed Commanding Officer, should have been placed on the retired list long before.'[19] The race issue would remain hugely important within the British West Indies Regiment: all officers were white and the NCO rank of sergeant was the highest obtainable for a 'coloured' man. It was indeed skin colour that made the difference. When asked in October 1917 whether commissions could be given to men 'not of pure European descent', the Colonial Office replied: 'The War Office have no objection to the grant to *slightly coloured gentlemen* [my *underlining*] of temporary commissions in British West Indies Regiment provided the candidates are British subjects and are considered in every other respect suitable to undertake the leadership of men'. It was at one point even specified that those who were 'one-sixteenth and one-thirty-second Negro' should not be excluded.[20] At least in the 9th Battalion one black Jamaican, Ivan Shirley, a former pupil of Dulwich College, was eventually made a lieutenant.*

Having non-white men giving orders to white men would, however, always remain an issue. When during the war the army began to run short of doctors, non-white doctors were commissioned with the rank of captain. Étienne Dupuch remembered how their West Indian 'coloured' doctor objected against the battalion's commanding officer's order to move camp to a nearby site which the medic considered unhealthy. Resenting the rebuff by a black man, the colonel stuck by his order and the result was a day long tug-of-war between the two and this while the men were effectively moving camp. In the end the colonel gave in after the doctor had threatened to report him for any sickness that would break out in the new camp and, though in the

---

* Ivan Shirley eventually became an assistant to fellow-Jamaican and well-known campaigner for racial equality Dr Harold Moody in South London in 1928.

meanwhile it was well after dark, the men were ordered to return to the original location.

Apart from skin colour, there were other racial considerations that did play a role in the management of the British West Indies Regiment. The War Office had informed the Colonial Office in August 1915 that it did not want (East) Indians in the British West Indies Regiment, yet forty-one Indian volunteers from Trinidad had arrived with the first contingent in England. As they did not speak English and as problems regarding food requirements were expected, most were repatriated. Only those who were born in the West Indian colonies, could speak English, and would accept standard British rations could be accepted. Contrary to the aforementioned Indians, some native Americans from British Honduras or British Guiana actually matched the grade and did serve in the regiment.

If not the colour bar, then at least the paternalist attitude of the white elite was felt in other ways too. Lady Mallet, the wife of the British consul in Panama, Sir Claude Mallet, not only sponsored a Lady Mallet Panama Room and Costa Rica Reading Room in the still existing Star and Garter Home for Disabled Sailors and Soldiers in Richmond, but also published a collection of letters, 'principally by the coloured West Indians who volunteered in Panama'.[21] While most letters are expressions of gratitude for receiving comforts such as chocolate and tobacco, it is particularly striking these letters from later drafted, lesser educated men have all been reprinted with their original grammatical and spelling errors. It raises the question what was the ultimate purpose of this publication: self-praise for Lady Mallet's charity or exposing the West Indians as an underdeveloped species, well looked after by benevolent Brits? In striking contrast with Lady Mallet's publication are the two autograph books of Miss E. Burton, a nurse who worked at the local hospital in Seaford when the West Indian contingent was housed there for training in 1915, now preserved in the Imperial War Museum.[22] Here, the poems, letters, and dedications written by West Indian soldiers from the earlier, relatively better educated contingents are all in nearly faultless English and quite often in beautiful handwriting. As the drawings depicting British lions and mockeries of the Kaiser, their words give expression to the patriotism and determination to fight of the West Indians:

> We'll surprise William the Kaiser
> With our bayonets sharp as razor
> And then he'll know at once
> That we are the West Indians

Thus wrote Private John Henry Lyken. Yet, the same autograph books also witnesses a curse that would remain with the West Indians throughout their stay in Western Europe: the chill. Private Jacob S. Cunningham who was suffering from pneumonia, wrote in nice and clear script on a loose paper dated 9 October 1915:

> For I am cold, cold, cold, boys
> Cold in my hands and hair
> In my mouth and my nose
> From my eyes to my toes
> And even the clothes I wear.[23]

The striking difference between Lady Mallet's publication of letters with all its spelling mistakes and the beautiful English in nurse Burton's autograph books is also a reflection of the different compositions of the West Indian contingents: while the first to arrive were composed of well-educated and by consequence language-savvy men, the later drafts were mainly composed of manual labourers, such as men who had worked on the Panama Canal or on banana plantations.

The cold that private Cunningham was referring to was partly due to the shoddy and inadequate accommodation in the Seaford camp, and as a consequence 'hospitals in the locality were filled to overflowing' with sick BWIR men. Between 20 October 1915 and 30 January 1916 nineteen West Indians succumbed in Seaford. The situation was even worse in Withnoe near Plymouth, where the 3rd and 4th battalions were sent for training around the turn of the year. Besides lacking enough warm clothing, the men in Plymouth were housed in tents because of shortage of huts. Between January 1916 and February 1917 twenty-eight of them died.

It was in the camp at Seaford in October 1915, shortly after their arrival in Britain, that the West Indians demonstrated their agency for the first time. When besides the cold and the rain they had to suffer due to unsuitable housing conditions, the pay was delayed, some mounted a public protest. Led by Henry Somerset, an engineer and ex-policeman from British Guiana, and several Trinidadians, a group of men refused to appear on roll call and the text 'No Money, No Work' was chalked on a wall. 'Old Colonel Barchard' reacted swiftly: he had their uniforms confiscated and the men were immediately repatriated in their civilian clothes. Barchard's response was in fact quite moderate as he could have easily categorized the event as mutiny, a delict that was punishable with death. Probably he took into consideration the fact that the protesters were a small minority, had indeed suffered not only during transport but also by the housing conditions and that as volunteers they were not acquainted with military life and customs, and had thus reacted as they would have in civil life.

On the initiative of Secretary of State for the Colonies Bonar Law, a West Indian Contingent Committee was formed towards the end of 1915. The key figures all had substantial experience as colonial officers in the Caribbean, and all had a direct link with the Colonial Office. Its task was to look after the welfare of the Caribbean soldiers overseas, both through policy and through material aid. Hence, after a visit of some well positioned committee ladies to the camp and hospital in Seaford, warm clothing such as socks, warm underwear, and gloves were provided. The committee equally sent the BWIR men comforts such as cigarettes, Christmas presents, games, cricket and football requisites, and each battalion was provided with musical instruments for a drum and fife band. The Committee's role was certainly not without importance: for the West Indian soldiers who after all were unable to go on leave, such comforts did matter. It was also the West Indian Contingent Committee that had the distinctive cap badge for the British West Indies Regiment designed, produced, and kitted out. Depicting Columbus' ship under the British Tudor Crown and surrounded by a laurel and palm wreath, the emblem which also adorns BWIR graves in First World War cemeteries, can be considered a success. Combining the crown with wreaths and a ship, it was a clear, dignified, but also neutral design, unlike for instance the badge of the New Zealand (Māori) Pioneer Battalion which stressed the subordinate labour nature of that unit by showing pickaxe and axe but also the chained head of tattooed Māori (especially the chain was so disliked that many members removed it from their badge). The fact that one badge was chosen for the whole regiment and that each man, whether officer or private, was given one made it moreover a highly identifying and unifying object. And this was precisely one of the political objectives of the West Indian Contingent Committee: not only to strengthen the bond between the Empire and its West Indian servicemen, but also to bolster a sense of West Indian groupness among the rank and file. Working within the still existing West India Committee – formed as a lobby group for British-based merchants and absentee plantation owners with business interests in the Caribbean – the West Indian Contingent Committee, was obviously a highly paternalist endeavour. When it successfully argued not to exclude the BWIR men from YMCA huts and estaminets, the committee stressed that the West Indian rank and file 'though generally of colour' were of a 'different educational and social status from the West Africa and some other soldiers from the Crown Colonies', camouflaging in this discourse the essential boundaries of race and skin colour with notions of class distinctions.[24]

By April 1916 from the contingents that had arrived from the West Indies, three battalions had been formed and trained in Seaford and Plymouth from whence they were sent to Alexandria where some months later they were joined by a fourth battalion. Though trained and armed they were not used as combat troops but deployed along the Lines of Communication. It was even discussed whether the BWIR should be converted into pioneer battalions. As this would be heavily resented by the men themselves and by the population in the West Indies, the proposal was rejected. Yet, even without a formal change of its mission and titles, the BWIR men must have felt aggrieved about their subordinate role. The chance of catching the Kaiser as the Jamaican volunteers sang, would not be theirs and wasn't even seriously considered: on 23 January 1917 the War Cabinet received a report from the War Office stating that the British West Indies Regiment had done well carrying ammunition along the Lines of Communication but that they had not received good reports as frontline soldiers, which was an odd statement taking into account they had thus far never been used in this role.[25] C.L.R. James called it 'the old story of the black man being first refused an opportunity to be afterwards condemned for incapacity'.[26] Eventually, on the persistent demand of its commanding officer, Lt Colonel Wood-Hill, the 1st battalion was allowed to be engaged in battle and would be so in Egypt and Palestine as from the summer of 1917. It would, however, remain the only battalion of the British West Indies Regiment to have been given a combatant role.

In total between 15,000 and 16,000 men were recruited and eleven battalions were sent overseas, four of which were infantry battalions, one reserve battalion and seven labour battalions. An overview of their designation and service overseas as well as their composition is given in appendix 1. All battalions were mixed, i.e. with recruits hailing from different British possessions in the Caribbean, but some were more mixed than others: while the 8th Battalion took on contingents from Trinidad, Grenada, Barbados, British Guiana, St Lucia, St Vincent, the Leeward Islands and Jamaica, the 6th Battalion seemed to have been fairly homogenous Jamaican. The strength of the units could obviously differ according to the losses it had undergone and other circumstances. When the 8th Battalion arrived at Caestre in Northern France on the 2 August 1917, it counted twenty-three officers and 992 other ranks, which is roughly the same as a British infantry battalion at full establishment. When it left Flanders on Christmas Eve 1917, the strength was diminished to seventeen officers and 651 other ranks.

With 10,000 out of some 15,000 men, two thirds of the British West Indies Regiment were Jamaican. The second largest group consisted of recruits from Trinidad and Tobago: some ten per cent while Barbados and British Guiana accounted for about five per cent of the BWIR men. The other colonies accounted for one and half per cent (Leeward Islands) to three and a half per cent (British Honduras) of the regiment. If we compare the population figures of the colonies in 1914 with the number who served in the British West Indies Regiment, we see that only in Jamaica and British Honduras more than one per cent of the inhabitants joined. Especially the case of British Honduras is remarkable as this was one of the smaller, poorer, and relatively more remote colonies, yet it contributed a relatively higher share of its population to the British West Indies Regiment. For Barbados, generally considered the most British of the Caribbean islands, we see a reverse phenomenon with a participation below half a per cent. It is, however, difficult to make conclusions solely based on these figures. Not only are they approximate and relatively small compared to other Imperial contributions in manpower, but many variables have to be taken into account. Practicalities such as transport issues (lack of money or lack of ships) might have prevented potential recruits to join, while from British Guiana many recruits were sent back home suffering from tropical diseases. British Guiana and Trinidad and Tobago, colonies who contributed relatively fewer men according to the size of their population, had large (East) Indian communities who were not allowed to join the West Indian Contingents. Finally, the multitude of motivations (patriotism, unemployment, political…) why 'coloured' inhabitants of the Caribbean colonies decided to join up also prevents reaching any conclusions as to the pro- or anti-war attitude of the different colonies' populations.

According to Algernon Aspinall in Charles P. Lucas' semi-official history of the British Empire in the Great War, of the more than 15,000 who served in the British West Indies Regiment, 185 were killed or died of wounds, while 1071 died due to sickness. His figures, based on those of the West Indian Contingent Committee of which he had been the secretary, were frequently copied and quoted but do not match with the official figures of the Commonwealth War Graves Commission (CWGC). This body registered 1397 men of the British West Indies Regiment who died on service between 1915 and 1921. The figure declines to 1345 if we consider the end of the war (signing of the Versailles Treaty, 28 June 1919) or to 1153 if we consider the Armistice on the Western Front (11 November 1918) as terminus ante quem. Apart from some individuals who died during transport in places such as Bermuda, Gibraltar, or Malta, we notice that of the 1397 BWIR men in the CWGC's database, 105 died in the West Indies, while 124 are commemorated in the United Kingdom – a figure which includes those who died and were buried on sea. Italy where some of the battalions spent the winter of 1917 – 18 and where the whole BWIR was concentrated after the Armistice counts for 157 casualties. If we look at the main theatres where the BWIR was deployed during the war, we see that 142 are now commemorated in Egypt and half a in Israel-Palestine, making a total of 221 for the Middle Eastern front. The bulk, however, died on the Western Front: 703, of whom 522 in France and 181 in Flanders. In the next chapter, I will analyze more in detail those who died in Flanders.

These figures belie the assumption made by many that the Middle East (Egypt and Palestine) was the major war theatre for the British West Indies Regiment, a supposition clearly enhanced by the fact it was the only front where West Indians have had a combatant role. With seven out of the twelve battalions serving in France and Flanders and counting for over half of the casualties in the British West Indies Regiment, the importance of the Western Front in the West Indian war experience is obvious.

Chapter Three

West Indians in France and Flanders

After only a brief sojourn in Egypt, the 3rd and 4th battalions of the BWIR returned to Europe towards the end of August 1916. They would later be joined in France and Belgium by five other battalions whom in contrast to the 3rd and the 4th were from the outset designated as service, i.e. labour battalions. Most of these later recruited battalions arrived directly from the Caribbean in Brest, sometimes welcomed by the local population in a manner not unlike the magnificent way the Indian Army Corps had been received in Marseilles in September 1914: while marching to the railway station accompanied by a French band, 'the inhabitants of Brest gave a great reception throwing flowers and sweets to the men', the clerk of the 7th Battalion wrote on 19 June 1917, only two days before the men would arrive at their final destination and would be subject to their first bombardment.[1] The 9th Battalion on the other hand, had arrived in England and travelled by train from west to east, taking another boat landing them in Boulogne. Their reception was contrasted with how they had been welcomed in England, so chaplain Horner wrote: 'Absent was the attention, gone were the smiling faces, and absent, too, were the cheers of welcome'.[2] The townsfolk of Boulogne had obviously seen much more 'dusky lads' (as Rev Alfred Horner called them) and had experienced the war from much more closely than their fellow countrymen in Brest.

The duties assigned to the West Indians in Western Europe were mainly loading, transporting, and unloading ammunition, but also digging trenches and all kinds of construction works, such as building artillery positions. It has been alleged that especially the 3rd and 4th battalions with trained infantrymen, were deployed close to the frontline assisting the batteries and feeding the guns, but their war diaries prove that they were also used in a large variety of menial tasks. The 3rd Battalion, for instance, spent most of the autumn and winter of 1916–17 working in the docks in Boulogne. At the same time, a battalion that was from the outset designated for labour, could also serve close to the frontline: at the end of August 1917 the 7th Battalion had men working at Marengo Dump (near Essex Farm), at 5km from the front-line North of Ypres, and in October 1917 it even had working parties on the 'Advanced Field Artillery Positions'. Sometimes more grisly tasks fell to the West Indians. A detachment of Étienne Dupuch's 4th Battalion once had to repair a section of a communication trench that had collapsed after a German barrage. Their picks were ploughing through the bodies of men who had been killed and were buried when the trench fell in.

All this was important work, yet the exclusion from combat service was considered a racial slur and deeply resented. It was something that the officers noticed as well. Rev Alfred Horner wrote how 'when we hear that coloured soldiers in other armies have shown remarkable aptitude in the attack, we, who are in the know, feel certain that the same desire to be personally "in at the thing" animates our boys too'. Despite being denied combat experience, soldierly display and military behaviour remained hugely important for the West Indians. The padre who served as a chaplain with the 9th Battalion – recruited as service troops – described how smart ceremonies of 'changing of the guard' were organized in the villages where they resided. The battalion's band played not only established military tunes and marches, but also had new ones composed, to which titles were given of the places they 'had visited in France' [sic] such as 'Poperinghe', 'Ondank' (both in Belgium) or the 'Tannery March'. Yet, they also played the music from home and the memory of hearing 'Farewell, my sunny home' played 'through the historic ruins of shell-swept

Ypres', made the song 'sacred' in the chaplain's opinion and he urged his Bahamian readership never to cut the song out of programmes.

The portrayal of the West Indian rank and file, even from his service battalion, as soldiers and behaving alike, is ubiquitous in Rev Alfred Horner's sketches. When a platoon of fellow Bahamians marched into a village singing, and approached the *Mairie* and the Town Major's office, 'a brisk order is given; there is silence in the ranks, rifles are correctly sloped, the step is brisk and quickened'.[3] Especially the mention of the rifles is not without importance: it appeared that even when used as labourers, the men who presumably belonged to the 4th Battalion (which had been trained as soldiers and comprised many Bahamians) were allowed to keep their personal arms. In a moving sequence of the documentary film Mutiny, Jamaican Clifford Powell, at 110 in 1999 allegedly the British Army's oldest known First World War veteran, not only remembered but also demonstrated on camera how the colonel and the captain were saluted, using his walking stick for a rifle.

At the same time, British officers, including Rev Alfred Horner, remained sceptic regarding the military qualities, and especially the discipline, of their own unit. In a sentence which demonstrates his British paternalist view on 'his boys', Horner judged: 'As long as soldiering meant bands and uniform and a certain element of mild heroism all was well; but when it meant smartness, neatness and, above all, punctuality – a thing the West Indian knows but slightly – and, again "not answering back-" for he loves to argue, it was not so well.' While most of their white officers seem to have been to a certain degree sympathetic to the interests and desires of the West Indian rank and file, not seldom a paternalist and condescending tone betrayed their innermost conviction of white superiority. Without saying it with so many words, Rev Alfred Horner, for instance, demonstrates in his writings how he considered the black soldiers of the 9th Battalion as childlike, not unlike the dominating view in France of the *tirailleurs sénégalais*. Horner consistently calls them throughout his book 'our boys' and with clear pleasure he writes how when working with the heavy guns, they had an 'insatiable desire' to pull the cord which fires the gun and how, sometimes after some bargaining, they would often be allowed to do so. The fact that he is in a peculiar sense the author of the devastating noise which follows seems to create in *le soldat noir* a certain sense of satisfaction'. Whereby the use of the French term is even more recalling of the well-known French view of their African soldiers as big playful boys. The same author, however, also stresses the fact that his 'boys' were 'drawn from the public-school teacher class in many of the W.I. colonies.' And, when the 9th Battalion resided in a certain area where the authorities had banned all 'coloured' labour troops from visiting cafés and YMCA huts and had this order extended to the BWIR men on the grounds that they did the work of labour troops, their officers successfully appealed to General Headquarters stating that the men had been enlisted to fight and were armed and equipped as soldiers and therefore had all the privileges as such, no matter what duties had been demanded from them.[4] All in all, this somewhat ambiguous attitude of the British officer towards his West Indian rank and file was not unlike that of his counterpart in the Indian Army: a certain degree of sympathy and genuine appreciation for their military and/or intellectual capacities whereby the men's interests would be defended, yet at the same time stressing their 'Otherness' and thus inequality. With the West Indians as with the Indians, it was ultimately skin colour that defined their otherness: the men but being not white, full equality was unimaginable.

Other officers were plainly harsh. Étienne Dupuch, serving in C Company of the 4th Battalion, described his commanding officer, Captain George Dawson, as 'the headman of a large cane plantation in Jamaica, where it was clear he was used to treating men like animals'.[5] Worse still, was Major Reginald Elgar Willis (Bildeston, 1887 –

Canterbury, 1956), the commanding officer of the 6th Battalion, who rightfully had the reputation of being a brute. Willis did not belong to the Jamaican plantocracy. The son of a Baptist minister in England, Willis had been in Jamaica since 1912 only, working as a schoolmaster in Westmoreland. When he joined in December 1916, Willis was given the rank of lieutenant, but little over three months later, he was already appointed major and temporary colonel, a very swift climb in the military hierarchy that corroborates C.L.R. James' statement about the inferior quality of many BWIR officers. One of the stories told about Willis was that he once had dug his spurs into the bandaged legs of a frostbitten man who had not sprung up to salute him. When the suffering man painfully struggled to his feet and hobbled away, the colonel was heard saying to a sergeant: 'When you write your mathi [mother] mountain back in Jamaica, tell the folks I'm turning Jesus Christ out here. I'm making the lame walk'.[6] Willis' behaviour aroused protest and riots, and this even before the battalions were moved to Taranto, where he would be among the officers triggering a mutiny when he ordered West Indian men to clean the latrines used by Italian labourers.

Despite being organized in battalions – and for the 3rd and 4th battalions also being trained in a fighting capacity – it is a striking fact that none of the West Indian battalions was actually deployed in this formation. Each of the battalions who served in France and Flanders and of which a war diary has been preserved was split up, not only in companies but often even in much smaller detachments such as platoons to provide 'the usual working parties' wherever required. Often, they were put at work far from their commanding officers and comrades. A case in point is the 3rd Battalion in early May 1918 when it had its headquarters in Putney Camp, Proven (Belgium). Of its C Company two platoons were at work in Hondeghem, one in Ebblinghem and one in Blendecques (France) – respectively some 20, 30, and even 40km from HQ! In early November 1918, still based in

Proven, 3/BWIR had working parties dispersed in an area stretching from Vlamertinghe (Belgium) to Armentières (France), a distance of more than 20km, and at the end of the month A Company was in its entirety in Dadizele and D Company in Beitem, while B Company was split up between Moorslede and Lendelede (all in Belgium), and C Company even had men in no lesser places than Caestre, Bailleul and Tourcoing (all in France). Thus the battalion's parties were spread over a zone of roughly some 100km^2!

Splitting up battalions is highly detrimental for the corps spirit and thus for the well-being of military personnel. This was certainly not less so for the West Indians. On the contrary, it might have been depressing to realize, and this not only for the 'real' soldiers of the 3rd and 4th battalions, that they were considered 'just' a labour reserve that was split up and put to use whenever and wherever military necessities (or the personal whim of a commanding officer) required. After all, this was a group to whom the emancipation from slavery was not only an important identifying factor but had even been a stimulant to support the British war effort.

The discriminatory treatment of the West Indian soldiers in Europe was not restricted to the fact they were designated a non-combatant role, despite those in the 3rd and 4th battalions being trained soldiers. In a private letter from Chaplain Harry Brown of 10/BWIR to the West Indian Contingent Committee in London, the minister complained that he had 'discovered German prisoners warm and comfortable, their rooms adequately heated by stoves and in the same barracks our West India boys on the extreme top floor without warming apparatus of any kind, cold and suffering.'[7] And suffer they did indeed. Eugent Clarke's 4th Battalion served on the Somme and at Ypres. More than eighty years later, the winter he spent on the Somme figured prominently in his memories of the war: 'We had to live under the earth. In dugouts. The Somme was bad, man. You stuck in the mud. We had a rough time in that country.

The wind would cut you. How we cold. How we cold. We had to wear double socks… Or the cold would have killed you'.[8] That winter – late 1916 and the early months of 1917 – was extremely harsh with months on end of negative temperatures, even causing the North Sea to freeze. After having spent the winter and spring of 1917 in the Somme, Clarke's 4th Battalion moved north, to support the British push in the Ypres Salient where the provisions to protect themselves against the elements would not be so much better…

That the accommodation in 1917 was inadequate for the men from the tropics is something that is both directly and indirectly apparent in the war diaries of the West Indian battalions. That of the 8th Battalion wrote just days after it had arrived near Ypres: 'Large number of cases of fever and chill as result of cold and exposure'. Despite this already being stated on 4 August 1917 and that most of August 1917 was exceptionally wet, the 8/BWIR men were still housed in tents on 30 August when the order was given to have the tents 'sandbagged'. And much worse, this seems to have been still the case in early December 1917 when due to snow and heavy frost the 'men suffered very much from the effects of the cold'. It is only on 6 December 1917 that a party was engaged in 'drawing tent-boards for the battalion' and that the men were issued with a third blanket. We see a similar situation with the 6th Battalion: upon their arrival at Pezelhoek, just north of Poperinghe, on 21 June 1917, the 6th Battalion was housed 'under canvass'. Yet, it is only on 14 December that the same war diary explicitly states that 'Huts are erected for the two companies on detachment at Vlamertinghe'. This certainly was not an unnecessary luxury. Still in December 1917, the 3rd Battalion's clerk wrote in Abele that 'Work is increasingly difficult owing to the increase in sickness due to a heavy fall of snow'.[9] It had by then daily sick parades where up to 150 men reported ill, a phenomenon which affected all West Indian units in Flanders!

Even a privileged officer as Chaplain Horner had reasons to complain. In his battalion's rest camp in Saint-Martin-Boulogne the tents were 'far from new' and he had to sleep 'with a waterproof sheet over us, and not under, to keep out the leakage from the thin canvas, whilst we lay in liquid mud'.[10]

Besides sickness, the battalions of the British West Indies Regiment obviously had their fair share of shelling and bombardments. As soon as the 3rd Battalion arrived at Bruloze near Loker (Belgium) on 25 May 1917 to assist the siege batteries at that location, they were subject to shelling resulting in fatalities. And barely one day after the 7th Battalion had arrived at its final destination near 'International Corner' on 21 June 1917, it was forced to move camp 2km further to Zwynland, not only due to the shelling but also because the men hadn't been issued gas masks yet.*

Shelling did also offer men denied a combatant role an opportunity to demonstrate their bravery: in the same battalion, on the night of the 7 November 1917 an incendiary bomb was dropped on Marengo Dump (near Essex Farm). Upon seeing how the explosion had set the camouflage nettings and boxes alight, one private Thomas woke up his comrades. With four others he then extinguished the flames, thus saving the dump. All this happened under a continuous heavy bombardment. A similar display of 'gallantry' was the act for which Lance Corporal Arthur Lawrence McLeod Henry of the 3rd Battalion was awarded a Meritorious Service Medal. When a dump caught fire under German shellfire and threatened to explode, Henry rushed to the scene. On 2 December 1918 Jamaican newspaper *The Daily Gleaner* published his account:

---

* International Corner was the name given to the crossroads of today's Eikhoekstraat-Legerweg-Westvleterseweg-Koekuitstraat, somewhat halfway between Poperinghe and Westvleteren. Until a decade or two ago the lettering 'International Corner' was still readable on the gable of a farm. Zwynland, not to be confused with the brewery of the same name in Poperinghe, is a location 2km more to the north, west of Westvleteren around today's Zwijnlandstraat. It is along the Zwynland Road that some weeks later the men of 7/BWIR would line to cheer King George on his way to or from the Abbey of Saint-Sixtus.

It was a narrow and marvellous escape, but I stuck it – myself, a sergeant by the name of England, one of our officers and a couple of Belgian soldiers – to the finish. Dozens got wounded and a few more were killed. The dump was being shelled. One of the shells hit in amongst a very large stack of shells and cartridges, all of a sudden with a great explosion that seemed to rent the earth. The dump began to go up and every man turned to his gas mask and shrapnel helmet. The majority started to run away, some stuck in their dugouts. Big shells were flying about in the air. I looked up the orderly room and had just left when a shell came through the roof. It was as dangerous running away as going to it. One fellow had already been killed running away. I felt like a man: my spirit was suddenly up and in a reckless way I dashed into the thick of it.[11]

The event described by Lance Corporal Henry probably happened on 10 July 1917, during the brief period the 3rd Battalion of the BWIR served on the Belgian coast. This is not only corroborated by the presence of the Belgian soldiers, but also by the existence of nine graves of men from the 3rd Battalion in cemeteries in the rear of the Nieuport front: eight graves in the British extension of the Belgian military cemetery Adinkerke Churchyard (graves 817–823 and 833), and one in Coxyde Military Cemetery (grave I.I.7).

Yet, not everyone was able to cope with the strain caused by the artillery fire and the stress. In October 1917 Private L. Jones of the 4th Battalion was admitted to hospital in Le Havre clearly suffering from shell shock: 'talking continuously and incoherently... partly religious and partly voicing his delusions of persecution... unduly emotional and he readily weeps...'.[12] That same month the 8th Battalion reported within a fortnight two men who went 'AWOL' (Absent Without Leave) and several cases labelled as 'NYDN' (Not Yet Diagnosed Nervous), the usual common denominator for shell shock cases awaiting further examination. The most dramatic case of these NYDN cases within the 8th Battalion occurred when the (white) Regimental Quartermaster Sergeant Maurice Dacre was found dead in his tent after a shelling in which twenty-two tents were perforated with shrapnel. Today, the grave of this 26-year-old Yorkshireman who had been detached from the Duke of Wellington's (West Riding) Regiment is to be found in Bedford House Cemetery (Enclosure No.4 grave II.E.7). Later the battalion would also be bombarded with mustard gas shells. And in the 9th Battalion, 17-year-old Herbert Morris was unable to stand the fire and ran off, a feat he would ultimately pay for with his life.

While there is no indication whatsoever that black servicemen were less able to endure the tension than their white colleagues, physicians overwhelmingly assumed this was the case. Hilary Buxton quotes the Freudian psychologist Henry Yellowlees who had seen 'more hysterical fits during one day spent among "insane" British West Indies Regiment soldiers than in the rest of his experience put together'. When he examined a group of West Indian soldiers who had been handcuffed to their beds in the mental compound of the Marseilles Stationary Hospital in 1919, he declared them 'not truly insane in our sense of the term, but cases of severe hysteria of a type unfamiliar amongst white men'.[13]

On 24 July 1917 the Scottish Major David Rorie MD, in charge of the 2nd Highland Field Ambulance (51st Highland Division), set up his headquarters in MDS (Main Dressing Station) Gwalia Farm, midway between Elverdinge and Poperinghe (Belgium) in preparation of the soon to start 3rd Battle of Ypres. In his war reminiscences published a decade after the war he devoted a paragraph to what he called a 'passing strange' scene:

> One evening a West Indian Labour Corps camp 'got it in the neck' from the bombing circus, and the place was suddenly

filled up with wounded niggers [sic]. Naturally emotional, and, equally naturally, scared to death, besides – in many cases – being badly injured, the black men made the dressing-room an inferno of shrieks, groans and cries which it was impossible to still. 'Hallelujahs' broke out sporadically in various places; one man started a Moody and Sankey hymn, the chorus being taken up in fits and starts by others till a rival tune from another corner bore it down. Outside the bombs kept crashing; we used a minimum of light though our windows were blanketed, in case of attracting attention; and as one gazed around the dim-lit hall of suffering at the gleaming teeth and rolling white eye-balls of the recumbent blacks on the operating tables and stretchers, the scene and the din, inside and outside, suggested an impromptu revival meeting in the nether regions, and called for the pencil of a Hogarth or a Breughel to do it justice.[14]

The fragment is interesting and highly revealing about the mentality of this highly ranked British officer. Being a doctor, Rorie was an educated man, yet this terrible account nearly overflows with stereotypes regarding Africans. He conceived them tellingly as 'West Indian Labour Corps' while the men were dressed in standard British uniforms, armed and trained soldiers (though employed as service units). Moreover, he bluntly calls them 'niggers', a pejorative and demeaning term unacceptable by many black people from the late 19th century onwards. That the author here has rather racist assumptions than merely one of colour, is clear from the sentences that follow. He does not seem to realize that 'shrieks, groans and cries' is not something inherent to 'black men' who are scared and 'in many cases-being badly injured' but would also occur when white men are heavily wounded and under constant bombardment. And instead of considering the singing of hymns during a heavy shelling as an act of morally supporting each other or even as bravery, he calls it 'a revival meeting in the nether regions', reinforcing the image of hell with its devils by stressing the 'gleaming teeth and rolling white-eyeballs'.

The scene Rorie described probably occurred on 29 July 1917 and concerned the 4th Battalion of the BWIR. Six men from the unit, hailing from Jamaica and the Bahamas did not survive and have been buried in Gwalia Cemetery, halfway between Poperinghe and Elverdinge. Seven others died later. Many decades later the horrible event was vividly remembered by Étienne Dupuch who had served in C Company of the battalion:

> The men were on parade in Belgium one day, ready to march off on a day's detail when shells from Passchendaele Ridge started falling in the area. ... As shells started inching nearer and nearer, Sergeant Sparkman ran out to the parade ground and told a Jamaican corporal in charge of the squad to dismiss the parade and let the men take cover. 'If Jesus Christ came down here today and told me to dismiss the parade', the corporal declared, 'wouldn't do it'. The blasphemy was hardly out of his mouth when a shell fell right in the middle of the parade and men went down like ten-pins in a bowling alley. When the smoke cleared Sparkman lay on the ground, his uniform spotless, but his head had been blown off from the shoulder by a piece of shrapnel....[15]

His memory didn't fail Dupuch: among the BWIR graves in Gwalia Cemetery, is that of Lance Sergeant Charles S. Sparkman, a white man from Nocatee, Florida, who had 'drifted into Nassau one day early in the war' (grave I.E.22). In contrast with Major Rorie's account, Dupuch also records a demonstration of extreme bravery and composure when a 'little Jamaican lance-corporal by the name of French' kept cool and almost single-handedly directed the operations to get the wounded into the hospital. Again, Dupuch is right. In the

1920 *Who's who in Jamaica* we read how corporal Leopold Ffrench of Ewarton was awarded the Military Medal for bravery on the Ypres Front.

The accounts of terrible shelling undergone by the West Indian rank and file in Flanders, induces us to take a closer look at the casualty figures of the British West Indies Regiment. They can tell us more on the whereabouts of a particular battalion and the nature of their deployment. In Belgium there are 181 graves of BWIR servicemen, and all died between 27 May 1917 and 26 August 1918. Of these fifty-two belonged to the 3rd Battalion and forty-three to the 7th Battalion. Of the other battalions present in Flanders, the casualty figures are considerably lower: Thirty in 6/BWIR, twenty-five in 4/BWIR, fourteen in 9/BWIR, eleven in 8/BWIR and two in 10/BWIR. The latter battalion probably did not stay long on Belgian soil and only arrived after the end of the Third Battle of Ypres, which explains for its low casualty figure. The one casualty registered as belonging to 1/BWIR is most probably a mistake as that battalion was never present in Belgium. All BWIR battalions who were present in Belgium served in the rear of the Ypres Salient, though, as we have seen, the 3rd Battalion also served on the Belgian coast, in the rear area of the Nieuport front in July 1917, at the period of the doomed Operation Hush. Further analysis of the CWGC registers reveal that while we usually have more personal details on the men of 4/BWIR, next-of-kin information on those of other battalions are more often lacking. A coincidence or a devoted clerk?

It also seems the number of casualties killed due to bombardments is much higher, at least for those buried in Flanders, than the often-quoted rate of died of diseases versus killed or died of wounds. This is corroborated by the fact that most died during the preparation or the course of the Third Battle of Ypres (summer–autumn 1917) and are buried in cemeteries more often associated with the location of batteries than with field hospitals (to which the sick were evacuated).

In France 522 BWIR casualties are commemorated of whom 186 lie buried in Mazargues Cemetery in Marseilles and eighty-eight in St Sever Cemetery in Rouen. Other cemeteries with an important number of BWIR graves are Boulogne (thirty-eight), Etaples (twenty-seven), Le Havre (twenty-one) and Wimereux (twenty-one). All are on the coast or far in the rear, so more probably related to sick and wounded cases. The figures are significant as they show the lethal importance of the front in Belgium to the BWIR: while more than half of the BWIR dead in France are buried (and hence died) on either the Mediterranean or North Sea coasts at a considerable distance of the frontline, those in Flanders died within the firing range of the German guns. Moreover, the figures are somewhat warped as most of the BWIR men who got ill or wounded in Belgium would have been evacuated to base hospitals in France so the real figure of casualties due to warfare in Belgium is certainly higher.

Also noticeable from the casualty figures is the high number of young men who served in the BWIR: while the eldest casualties of whom the age has been registered are 'just' 41 in Belgium and 48 in France (both were officers), there are not less than three 17-year-olds recorded in Belgium and the same number in France, the most tragic case being the executed Herbert Morris. Of more than half of the BWIR men, however, we have no information about the age at the moment of death, so the figures are not absolute, only indications.

The combined figures of both France and Belgium demonstrates once again the relative importance of the Western Front and question the established view of the importance of the Middle Eastern front for the BWIR: more than half, or 703 out of 1397 casualties registered by the CWGC fell in France and Flanders while the other fronts the BWIR was active on, account for respectively forty-seven (East Africa, graves in Tanzania and Kenya) and 221 (the Middle East – graves in Egypt, Israel and Palestine) registered deaths. In the U.K. 124 deaths have been recorded, including the ones who died at sea, while those who died in Italy and Malta, 160 men, were, apart from some individuals, probably mostly taken ill (a.o. influenza pandemic).

Eight men of the BWIR received a death sentence passed by military court during the First World War. Of these, four for the crimes of sleeping at post, striking a senior officer (2x), and mutiny were commuted in penalties of five to twenty years of penal servitude. In the four other cases the ultimate penalty was duly carried out, the men having been condemned for murder (2x), repeatedly striking a senior officer, and desertion. This means that half of the death sentences delivered to West Indian soldiers involved some kind of resistance against authority. A West Indian soldier had a much higher chance that the ultimate penalty was effectively carried out than any other Imperial group within the British Army, when we do not take into account the Chinese, Egyptian or African labourers who were 'mere' civilians subject to military law in matters of discipline. The figures are telling: 222 Canadians sentenced to death (twenty-five executed); 113 Australians (none executed); twenty-three New Zealanders (five executed); and eleven South Africans (one executed). Of the four executions of BWIR men, only one was carried out on the Western Front, and the victim was also the only West Indian to be shot for an offence not involving violence. Herbert Morris was just 17 when on 20 September 1917 he faced the firing squad in Poperinghe. The young Jamaican served in the 6th Battalion and had disembarked in France towards the end of April 1917, to arrive at Pezelhoek near Poperinghe on the 21 June where the men were housed in tents. His battalion was by then attached as corps troops to Ivor Maxse's XVIII Corps (Fifth Army) to handle ammunition. On 20 August 1917 while on his way to Essex Farm, just north of Ypres, Herbert Morris went absent without leave, only to be arrested soon after. During his court-martial on 7 September, he told the court that he could not tolerate the sound of gunfire, and that he had seen the medical officer but that the latter had not been able to help him. Despite a good character reference stating that Herbert Morris was considered to be of higher intelligence than most of his platoon comrades, he received the death sentence. It is not known whether the military authorities knew his true age, but if they didn't, it is clear they didn't consider enquiring about it. Herbert Morris might have been the youngest to have been Shot at Dawn during the First World War.* He is buried in Poperinghe New Military Cemetery (grave II. F. 45), eventually the CWGC cemetery with the highest concentration of shot-at-dawns but also the cemetery where Roy Manley, the brother of future Prime Minister Norman Manley was laid to rest.

Morris was court-martialled at the worst possible moment. Not only did the Third Battle of Ypres not go the way the British had hoped, but on 4 September 1917 two companies of the Egyptian Labour Corps had gone on strike following an air raid on Boulogne-sur-Mer. Two days later twenty-three Egyptians were killed when the protesting but unarmed labourers were fired on, an act repeated a few days later. And at roughly the same time Chinese Labour Companies near Dunkirk had gone into hiding and had refused to work following similar air raids. It is obvious that in such circumstances the British military authorities were quite nervous about the demonstrations of agency by what they considered 'native labour'. It is doubtful whether Herbert Morris would have been condemned to be shot, or his death penalty confirmed, if there had been no need to set examples.

The news of Herbert Morris' execution must have resounded throughout the West Indian battalions in Belgium and France. Long before those Shot at Dawn received public attention and without knowing his name, Étienne Dupuch pretty accurately referred to the affair in his memoirs, remembering seventy-five years after the events that it was a Jamaican that had run away under fire and that 'his last

---

* Herbert Burden, born 22 March 1898, was shot on 21 July 1915 and is certified the youngest, but as we do not have his exact birth date, Herbert Morris might very well be younger.

message to his mother was that he could not stand the soul-searing noise made by exploding shells'.¹⁶ It was something Dupuch, who had undergone and witnessed men's reactions in a violent bombardment, could perfectly understand.

Besides the rude behaviour of some officers and an overt or more discreet discriminatory treatment in matters such as work assignments, accommodation, or discipline, there are no plain reports of incidents of a racist nature before the Armistice (as opposed to the post-Armistice period) but some remarks in the sources hint at their occurrence. On 7 July 1918 the war diary of the 3rd Battalion mentions briefly: 'Friction with American troops in Watou' without detailing what the 'friction' meant.¹⁷ The Americans were the newly arrived 27th and 30th divisions of the American Expeditionary Force. While the 27th was recruited in the state of New York, the 30th was made up of Southerners from North Carolina, South Carolina, and Tennessee, not particularly men likely to mingle in a friendly way with black West Indians. Equally, we could wonder what treatment was meted out to the 100 men of the 6th Battalion's B Company who were detached to serve with the 75th South African Battery near Essex Farm in July 1917?

It also appears some of the West Indian units were at certain periods segregated and locked up in their camps. Jamaican born J. Ramson, padre of the 6th Battalion, wrote how his men were kept in a camp behind barbed wire upon arrival in France and how white tommies going on leave were chatting to them from the other side of the fence.¹⁸ Private Norris Roach wrote in a letter, published in the Grenadian newspaper *The West Indian* of 9 November 1917 how 'The _ _ children are very nice. They come around and throw chocolates and cigarettes to the boys, for we are not allowed to go out from camp. These children tell us all the news.' The ease of communication with the local children has also been noticed in the case of Indians and Chinese stationed on the Western Front, be it that with the West Indians language was probably less an issue. Though the only geographical specification mentioned in his letter is France, it is much more probable Private Roach was then based either in Belgium or near the French-Belgian border: not only his train journey from where they had embarked had taken two days and nights, but the men are able to converse easily with the children, something that was relatively easier to Flemish kids who had been living among English-speaking soldiers for nearly three years, than in most areas of France. Moreover, at the time he wrote his letter, all battalions of the BWIR were mainly active in Belgian Flanders, as is proven by the war diaries and West Indian graves. And after all, it was common, even for British soldiers, to designate the whole of the Western Front as 'France'. Yet, it was certainly through France he had travelled, a country with 'fields upon fields of wheat' which he, described as 'a lovely place, the houses both ancient and modern, are most beautifully situated. The poor peoples' houses are very tidily kept, and almost every house had a fine vegetable and flower garden'. It is almost as if Private Roach was echoing some of the descriptions of Europe we find in the censored letters the members of the Indian Army Corps sent home.

Even if Private Norris Roach and his comrades were at least at times not allowed to leave camp, segregation was not the usual custom for the West Indian rank and file. Bahamian private Étienne Dupuch relates in his memoirs how he was able to visit a camp and workshop of the Royal Engineers with one of their men whom he had befriended. What does appear, however, is that the number of local estaminets that could be visited by BWIR men was, at least at times, restricted and that this restriction was entirely due to the hybrid nature the British West Indies Regiment had in the eyes of the white decision-makers and this due to their skin colour. In the only surviving register of letters received by the Assistant Provost Marshal (APM) of Poperinghe, there is a loose page dated 19 July 1917. It states that the estaminet 'Breydel-De Coninck' (Duinkerkestraat 48) 'can be used for serving drinks to black troops, it [being] the only place where no females are employed', thus exemplifying the established practice within the British army of preventing non-white military personnel from engaging with white women. Men of the West Indian battalions visiting local cafés remained however a debated topic in Poperinghe as two other entries in the APM's register, both dated November 1917, demonstrate. In the first the commanding officer of the 9th Battalion BWIR asked what had been decided regarding the use of estaminets by men of his unit, and in the second his colleague of the 4th Battalion enquired whether the cafés 'In den Witten Hert' and 'In den Werkman' can be frequented by his men.[19] West Indians were surely allowed to visit local pubs, though the choice might have been restricted, and neither were they prevented of visiting local families. Rev Alfred E. Horner, the chaplain of the 9th Battalion, described how 'Before night-fall the little estaminets and coffee-houses will be found to contain these men, fraternizing in a wonderful way with the French civilians, telling them of their sunny homes in broken French, which they pick up quickly' or how they visited the locals at home 'huddled round the stove… doing odd jobs for the lady of the house, regaling themselves with coffee'. According to the priest, their friendly attitude earned them the soubriquet *'le soldat noir aimable'*. And when Étienne Dupuch, who was young and small, fell out on a march in France, the mother of a nearby farming family took pity on him and exclaiming *'petit garçon'*, she put her arm protectively around his shoulders, took him into her home and sat him down for a meal with the family.[20]

There was even opportunity for romantic engagements. Much to the consternation of the conservative *Clarion*, a Carib volunteer from British Honduras voiced in a letter home his intention to bring home from Europe a French woman. Étienne Dupuch was more restrained. The young Bahamian was fancied by a French girl whom he had met in a postcard shop. 'She didn't speak English and I didn't speak French, but for the rest of my stay in that town we met every afternoon in the shop and carried on a delightful conversation with the aid of a pocket French–English dictionary.' The romance, however, couldn't last and when the battalion was quite suddenly ordered to move up the lines, Étienne and his comrades marched past the shop. 'Standing at the window was my dream girl, whose name I have never learned. She waved. This was goodbye, forever. Tears were streaming down her cheeks.'[21]

It is clear that the local population could engage with the West Indians if they wished to. Probably due to the relatively small size of the British West Indies Regiment and their deployment relatively closer to the frontline, there are, however, hardly Flemish or French witness accounts on the West Indians. Yet, there is Father Achiel Van Walleghem, arguably the best diarist behind the front in Flanders. On 26 May 1917, he records where the recently arrived men of the British West Indies Regiment are in bivouac: 'On the farm of Alouis Adriaen and "Drie Goên" negroes have arrived to work'.* Van Walleghem was not sure of their provenance: in the manuscript of his diary he first noted: '(South Africans)' to replace it probably soon after by '(from West India – Jamaica)'. 'They are dressed like English soldiers; are civilized. Speak very softly, though are not much liked because of their sticky fingers, and the civilians prefer to see the back of them, because when they enter a place for a cup of coffee, they can stay anything from five minutes to a couple of hours.' So far, this note on the West Indians bears some similarities with the author's remarks when he witnessed the Indian soldiers two years previously. The West Indians are 'dressed

---

* The two locations Van Walleghem mentions are 3km apart of each other and, indeed, the companies of the newly arrived 3rd Battalion were billeted in different places: C and D companies remained at Bruloze (a hamlet at the foot of Kemmel Hill), while A company was in bivouac near Hallebast, Dikkebus (Alouis Adriaen's farm) and B company at the hamlet of Drie Goên (today Driegoenstraat, Reningelst).

like English soldiers' and 'are civilized. Speak very softly': here Van Walleghem marks a clear distinction with the North African *tirailleurs algériens* he had witnessed previously and whom on 9 December 1914 he had described as colourfully dressed and 'half savage', and while the mother tongue of the West Indians was English, the North Africans might have mastered just some words of French. Yet, even though according to the war diary the BWIR men had arrived not even two days before he wrote this very entry and that he considered them 'civilized', Van Walleghem states as a matter of fact that they have a propensity to steal ('sticky fingers') and that they easily linger on for hours. He ends his short paragraph on the West Indians noting that 'The blacks are terribly frightened of the bombardments. They stare shyly and haggardly when they hear a shell approaching and if it doesn't drop too far, they flee like possessed.'[22]

Despite the clearly xenophobic undertones and prejudices, Van Walleghem was not univocally negative. It even seems his established opinions were shaken when he got more personally acquainted with the men. For while the previous sentences could have been based on mere hearsay, the note he added at the foot of his entry of 26 May 1917 is certainly not: 'I have found a letter to one of those blacks written by his mother. What sincere, Christian, and motherly feelings! Not one of our mothers would say it better'. The latter sentence places the West Indians morally on the same footing as the Belgian civilians in the eyes of this village priest, and intellectually even on a higher level than some of his parishioners of which a minor but still considerable percentage was certainly illiterate. As in his dealings with Indians and Chinese, Van Walleghem comes to us as an inquisitive, even nosy, person who does not even refrain from reading letters to satisfy his curiosity in the 'Other' but also as one who is open to developing a more balanced view of the subjects of his study.

A day later Achiel Van Walleghem mentions how early in the morning Alouis Adriaen's farm was heavily shelled, reducing the buildings to ruins. While the Flemish inhabitants were safe in their cellars, the billeted West Indian soldiers fared less well: four were killed and three were wounded, according to Van Walleghem, a fact corroborated by the war diary of 3/BWIR. In the war cemetery closest to Alouis Adriaen's farm, La Clytte Military Cemetery in De Klijte, today five headstones with the crest of the BWIR (should) bear the date of 27 May 1917: the four casualties of the morning bombardment and one who was killed later that day.*

A third and final short mention of BWIR men in Van Walleghem's diary is dated 29 November 1917: 'Along the railway between the ammunition depot of Verhaeghe Farm and Schaapstal [east of Reningelst and north to southwest of the hamlet of Ouderdom] is a camp of blacks (West Indians). A great many of them are catholic, and some are serving in the artillery. We notice they smoke many cigars, while the other soldiers prefer cigarettes.'

Besides British comrades, American allies, or the local population, the West Indians could encounter more representatives of other peoples during their stay at the front in France and Flanders. Unfortunately, there is no known account of an eventual meeting between British and French West Indians at the front in France and Flanders. However, especially in 1918, soldiers from Guadeloupe, Martinique, and French Guiana were present at the front near Ypres when several battalions of the BWIR were also residing in the area. Had such a meeting occurred, it could have offered an interesting comparison between the two West Indian groups as black soldiers from the French territories in the Caribbean were, unlike their British brethren, integrated in the – mainly white – French metropolitan

---

* Graves II.A.15, II.B.18, II.D.13, II.D.14, and III.C.17. Two of the men, the corporals F.L.A. Dunn and A.C. Smith, had been for many decades wrongly registered by the CWGC as being killed on 26 May 1915. At the time of writing the mistake had already been corrected in the CWGC's database but not yet on the headstones.)

units and deployed for combat duties. It is a gap in our knowledge which may be somewhat illustrative, not only of the relatively large distance between the communities in the British and French Caribbean islands, but also of the fact that history writing is still largely a 'national' business with little room for comparative history, even within the same geographical area.

While there is little evidence of Caribbean prisoners of war in German captivity[23], there were frequent encounters with Germans, as German prisoner-of-war companies were often assigned similar tasks as the West Indians behind the British front. This did not always run smoothly. According to Rev Alfred Horner German prisoners frequently showed their dislike and disdain for the 'coloured' soldier and he relates to a particular instance when during a burial party 'a Bosche laughed at the poor dead forms on the stretchers and used terms unfortunately understood by the Inagua lads' whereupon a fisticuff developed between the Bahamians and the Germans.[24]

Equally little love was lost between the men from non-European labour units, especially the Chinese, and the West Indians, though Étienne Dupuch was shocked when he saw a group of Chinese labourers being driven at their work with sticks by British privates. The animosity between the BWIR and the CLC was, according to Rev Horner, partly due to the arrogant behaviour of the West Indians who stressed the fact that being soldiers they were more than mere labourers working for a wage. One source for trouble was, for instance, the fact that cafés and estaminets were out of bounds to all 'native' labour while the men of the BWIR were allowed in due to their military status. Frequently Chinese workers would be 'standing outside such places and making rather heated remarks as our boys, with, I daresay, an unnecessary amount of gusto, retired from their refreshment', so Horner writes.[25] In his book, the chaplain also refers to 'difficulties we used to have when quartered with

Chinese labour companies' though he does not give many details. These were probably far from the only incidents between Chinese and West Indians, though little has been reported. One exception is the Private 'Latrill' (probably a misspelling for Emanuel Latrelle, BWIR, Regt N° 12296) of Rev Alfred Horner's 9th Battalion who on 30 November 1917 complained to the Assistant Provost Marshal in Poperinghe that he had been 'spat in the face by a coolie'.[26] More important is the short entry in the war diary of the senior medical officer of the Lines of Communication in the Abancourt area about a fight between West Indian soldiers and Chinese labourers on 18 May 1919. Three Chinese were allegedly killed and one West Indian severely wounded. The Caribbean casualty, 43-year-old Jamaican Private Charles Henry of the 3rd Battalion, died one day later (Blargies Communal Cemetery Extension, grave V.E.1). This entry is equally important for the fact that it reminds us that in Spring 1919 not all West Indians were in Taranto waiting repatriation but that some units were still deployed in Europe clearing the battlefields.

And only one account relates to an encounter between a West Indian and an (East) Indian. On the ship taking them from Alexandria to France, Étienne Dupuch befriended a Sikh whose name he spelled seventy-five years later as "Hadrajasingh". According to Dupuch, he was a 'sergeant', probably a daffadar serving in the Indian cavalry. During a stop-over in Sicily, Dupuch was outraged when a 'small English private' pushed his tall and handsome Indian NCO friend away to take his place at the rail to trade with the farmers in the dinghies below. Restraining him from fighting, the Sikh told him: 'It is not for such as these that we fight, Dupuch, it is for the grand British ideal'. The Bahamian realized then and there 'that the lowest, scrubbiest Englishman was considered superior to the finest Indian'. Later, in France, he had a long night-time talk with another Indian on their inferior position in their own land, something he called 'a painful, almost unbelievable story'. Dupuch related the Indian situation to existing prejudices in the Bahamas and to forms of discrimination experienced by men in his regiment and, so he stated, he began to dream of being instrumental in breaking down racial barriers in the Bahamas, something that half a century later he would be able to realize as a member of his country's House of Assembly.[27]

Chapter Four

A Troublesome Demobilisation: Mutiny and Difficult Return

Having spent a long time side by side on transport, in camps, on the battlefield, in short being 'stuck in it together' and being treated alike, had to a certain degree unified the West Indians. The emergence of a particular West Indian awareness was noticeable and, as we have seen, had been from the outset one of the political objectives of the West Indian Contingent Committee. Yet, this 'West Indianness' was always related to how the West Indians perceived themselves in relation to others and how they were perceived by these others. Though living, meeting, talking, and getting to know each other had certainly enhanced mutual understanding, inter-island rivalry did not disappear: Grenadians complained that their island had to provide the men, while Jamaica and Barbados provided the officers, while Jamaicans had the impression they were disfavoured. This phenomenon of attraction and repulsion, of unifying tendencies and island nationalism is something that characterizes the region's history to this day, with – as remarkable climax – the short-lived political union as the West Indies Federation between 1958 and 1962.

The fact, however, that the BWIR men to a certain measure identified with a West Indian supra-nationality, became very clear during and after the famous Taranto mutiny. After the Armistice, some 8,000 men of the British West Indies Regiment who had been deployed in France and Flanders were concentrated in Taranto, the port where many of them had also spent the previous winter. Here, in the South of Italy, they would last out the colder months while awaiting their repatriation. In Taranto, the West Indians suffered from a change in attitude from their white comrades, and from the harsh treatment on behalf of some of the commanding officers, including the racist camp commander Brigadier-General Cyril Cary-Barnard. Eugent Clarke still loathed the man eighty years later: 'He was a rough man. South African. Oh Lord! With him you couldn't even go to the gate, much less go to town. I forgot his name. He was a rough man!'[1] Tellingly Clarke presumed the camp commander was South African. In fact, he was not: Brigadier-General Cary-Barnard was born in London and had climbed the ranks in the Wiltshire Regiment. However, he was a decorated veteran of the Boer War, and had served on the Western Front, being wounded, and mentioned in despatches, before being assigned the post of Base Commandant in Taranto in October 1917. In 1919, after the battalions from the Middle East had arrived, Captain A.A. Cipriani was able to form an opinion about Cary-Barnard, remembering later that the General 'stated that he had no intention of treating West Indians like British troops, that they were only niggers and better treated than any nigger had a right to expect'.[2] Indeed, Cary-Barnard had the West Indians described in all official orders as 'coloured natives' – something they were not – they were denied access to cinema and YMCA huts, and they were only allowed to go into town on certain conditions.

The treatment that was meted out to the West Indians in Taranto aggravated the resentment that had risen after it had become known that the War Office had denied the BWIR the general pay rise that had been granted to all other British regiments by Army Order 1 of 1918. It seems the straw that finally broke the camel's back was the order given on 6 December 1918 by the aforementioned brutish commanding officer of the 6th Battalion, Major Reginald Willis, to a party of BWIR servicemen to clean the latrines of Italian labourers. It surely was an insensitive and provocative act to order proud men who had volunteered to soldier and to whom the memory of slavery was very lively to clean the latrines of menial workers. The reaction came swiftly: that same night some men slashed his tent with bayonets, dispersing quietly afterwards. One day later, the 9th and 10th battalions refused to work, unrest spread, and open mutiny broke out. The rebellion lasted three full days. Then the whole regiment was disarmed.

Yet, neither the disarmament of the battalions, nor the trial of more than sixty men from the BWIR who had been involved in the mutiny, were enough to quell the unrest entirely. Only days after the mutiny, on 17 December 1918, a Caribbean League was formed, a short-lived organization designated by Richard Smith as 'a landmark in Anglophone Caribbean nationalism'.[3] From the outset its existence was known to the British authorities, who were kept informed. Mainly composed of NCOs, the League had the vague programme of working for the 'General Welfare' of the British West Indies. Yet, at a subsequent meeting of the NCOs of the 3rd Battalion much more revolutionary talk was heard: the outcry that 'the Black man should have freedom and govern himself in the West Indies and that force must be used, and if necessary, bloodshed, to attain that object', was loudly applauded and plans for a general strike to obtain higher wages were made. Smith points out to the fact that the League was predominantly composed of sergeants, thus claiming political leadership, whereas the mutineers were nearly all private soldiers. All leaders were Jamaican and had planned to base the organization's headquarters in Jamaica, something the Trinidadian sergeant who was the authorities' informer, objected to. Thus, Smith states, the League anticipated the future juxtaposition of pan-West Indian anti-colonial movement and island chauvinism or in the words of Joseph: 'the bond forged on the battlefield was the first victim of peacetime provincialism'.[4] Yet, the formation of the League shows the emergence of a political Afro-Caribbean consciousness out of their war experiences, the realization that the only way forward was to fight for civil rights for black people and the intention to continue the struggle after demobilization.

West Indian unity was also shown in the more formal protest that was mounted against the exclusion from the general pay rise. During the mutiny a petition was prepared in which 180 sergeants stated that this discrimination was not only an affront to men who had volunteered to fight for the Empire but also an insult to the whole of the West Indies. Among the signatories were representatives from the different colonies and the letter was sent to the Governors who forwarded it to the Colonial Office by February 1919. The mutiny, the continuous protests, and the clear display of unity among the West Indian rank and file did not miss their effect: after similar requests by the West Indian Contingent Committee and colonial officials, the War Office climbed down and retroactively granted the BWIR men what they would have been entitled to a year previously, had they not been considered 'natives'. That this decision was prompted by anxiety for the consequences of a continuous discrimination, rather than by a belated sense of justice and goodwill, is obvious.

In both London and the Caribbean territories, the authorities must have been aware of the ongoing politicisation within the British West Indies Regiment. For in the first half of 1919, with more free time at hand and still being out of their country on something that was considered a mission for higher ideals, the West Indian soldiers in Europe exchanged newspapers, commented upon them, and discussed ideas for the improvement of the colonies. In late spring 1919, a Grenadian wrote to newspaper editor T.A. Marryshow, a proponent of West Indian Federation, congratulating him on his pleas for representative government: '…it was our intention to invite our countrymen to take that step as soon as we returned home. Our present experience has opened our eyes more widely to the disadvantages which our little colony has to contend with. When the papers reached us out here they were lent to the men of different islands and often [when] reading the speeches they were filled with great enthusiasm'.[5]

Not only in Taranto, but also in England West Indian soldiers were concentrated to await demobilization and repatriation. In his 1937 memoirs *A Long Way from Home* the famous Jamaican poet and novelist Claude McKay (15 Sep 1889–22 May 1948), one of the figureheads of the so-called Harlem Renaissance, as the explosion of African American culture in the 1920s has been called, remembered how he had been a regular visitor to the 'club for coloured soldiers' in Drury Lane, London, where he had listened to the soldiers telling tales of their war experiences. Many of them were interested in what African Americans were thinking and writing, so McKay brought with him to the club copies of magazines and newspapers such as Du Bois's *The Crisis* or Garvey's *Negro World*. After a soldier from Jamaica had invited him to visit the demobilization camp at Winchester, McKay wrote a series of articles about the 'coloured' soldiers and their club, which were published in *Negro World*, the organ of Garvey's UNIA. When the magazine with the first article arrived at the Drury Lane club, the Englishwoman in charge took exception and McKay became persona non grata: McKay had interviewed her, quoting what she had told him about her 'coloured boys' and their virtues 'if white people knew how to manage them', adding that she had a patronising white maternal attitude towards her 'coloured' charges.[6] Soon after, McKay's attentions shifted to the International Club, where the radicals met and where he was introduced to Marxist thought. While initially he was the only African Caribbean visiting, he soon introduced others, including three soldiers he had met in the Drury Lane Club.

As McKay's case demonstrates, the West Indian presence in Europe during and immediately after the Great War had an important influence on policymakers such as Pan-Africanist activists. But such influence quite often went in two ways. While listening to their experiences and telling a mainly African American public about it, McKay introduced the West Indian soldiers to Black activist papers and radical left thought, not only in the London clubs but also in the camp at Winchester. There the influence the radical papers had on the residing West Indians was reinforced by the presence in the same camp of white Americans, to whom racial segregation was the order of the day. It was written in the stars that troubles would develop and during a fight between the two groups on 29 April 1919, an American soldier was wounded. Subsequently, the West Indians marched into Winchester, armed with sticks, and haranguing any passing US serviceman. The Winchester unrest was widely reported in both the provincial and the national press.

Other events in 1919 must have further galvanized the African Caribbean view on their British overlords and their own situation of subordination. In Britain, where according to David Killingray the black population had probably doubled to some twenty thousand people by the end of the war,[7] men from Arabian, Asian, and African descent had become the scapegoats for soaring unemployment and other problems due to the demobilization and throughout 1919 violent race riots took place in a number of seaports. Trinidadian Felix E.M. Hercules (1888–1943), the secretary-general of the London-based Society of Peoples of African Origin who was to tour Jamaica later in 1919 was among those campaigning against the racial attacks. Though none of the racial violence in Britain was directly targeted against non-white ex-servicemen, some veterans were caught up in them. At the same time, during what has been coined the Red Summer, in more than thirty-five cities in the United States African Americans were violently attacked and, at least in the case of Chicago, fought back. Here, black soldiers were particularly targeted: at least ten of seventy-seven black people lynched that year in the USA were veterans in uniform.

To the black veterans, it must all have been utterly shocking. Was this the gratitude and justice they could expect for having served the motherland?

The colonial authorities were terrified by the pre-revolutionary climate developing in the West Indian battalions and before their return precautions were taken. By the time the first contingents reached home, British battle cruisers were on stand-by in the Caribbean and local garrisons had been strengthened. On most islands the soldiers were not given a heroes' welcome by the white elite, something that was visibly still hurting Eugent Clarke towards the end of his life: 'They never gave us a welcome like how the Bahamas welcomed their soldiers when they came back. They said that West Indians may riot in town or something. Because they are a riotous people'.[8] In the Bahamas, though even if the returning men were welcomed as heroes, not all was well. Étienne Dupuch relates how soon rivalry developed between the ex-servicemen and the police because the local girls left their policemen-friends and went for the returned soldiers. A consequence was that for the slightest infraction of law the soldiers were brutalized by the police while the free liquor handed out to them turned some of them into alcoholics.

Rumours abounded that veterans intended to incite a rising of the black population in Jamaica and that anti-colonial agitation was expected to spread throughout the West Indies. A telegram warning of such a general insurrection was sent by Viscount Milner, Secretary of State for the Colonies, to all West Indian governors on 3 July 1919. Though a large, general rebellion did never materialize, here and there throughout the Caribbean riots broke out. In Jamaica, on 18 July 1919, discharged seamen and ex-servicemen were involved in a brawl with British seamen and white civilians and the ex-servicemen were heard chanting 'Kill the whites'. One day later, coinciding with the Peace Day celebrations everywhere in the British Empire, the returned soldiers of Trinidad were supposed to lead a victory parade in Port of Spain. Yet only 130 joined the procession. A large number of ex-servicemen, either in uniform or in civvies, merely looked on or booed. The police believed the protest was due to the fact they hadn't been allowed to carry arms, something that had been forbidden out of fear they would shoot their officers. Most probably an overreaction fuelled by the authorities' anxiety for the veterans' radicalism and activism, it obscured the real cause of their grievances which rather had more to do with the treatment they had received overseas and the local government's land settlement scheme for the returned BWIR men than with the refusal to carry arms.

Unlike in most other Caribbean colonies, the returning soldiers were given a grand welcome in British Honduras. Upon disembarkation in the capital of Belize on 9 July 1919 they paraded under banners and flags to government house where they were addressed by Governor Eyre Hutson. As the representative of the Imperial government, he promised them they would receive the remaining portion of their pay as soon as possible and explained the government's land settlement scheme for ex-servicemen. Yet, within days the good spirits vanished, allegedly after the Garveyite-friendly local newspaper *The Independent* had reported on the violence against black people in England and Wales. On the night of 22 July, returned soldiers marched through the streets of the town, armed with sticks and breaking shop windows. The fact they spread out strategically on street corners, communicating with verbal instructions and whistle blasts suggested a well-planned demonstration of power. They were soon joined by comrades and civilians, and the mob increased to some 3,000 to 4,000 men, women, and children – between a quarter and a third of the town's population. Shops were looted and white inhabitants were threatened, ridiculed and in some cases beaten. The violence was perpetrated by both returned ex-servicemen and civilians and very explicitly directed against the white population. During a meeting the next day – there were no arrests out of fear of aggravating the situation – a committee of the ex-servicemen led by Samuel A. Haynes (about whom more in the next chapter), raised issues connected to their personal improvement, but also asked to introduce fixed prices to combat economic dearth. Symbolically important was the decision that it would be the black ex-soldiers who maintained order in the town to bring the looting under control, something the Governor regarded as a humiliation to the authorities. In the words of Haynes, ten years after the event: 'It was I whose appeal to sobriety a reason saved the handful of Europeans in Belize from a savage massacre when the returned soldiers rioted in an orgy of rum in the summer of 1919... I rose to the occasion and silenced the radicals'.[10] In the Belize riots the civilians who were suffering under an economic crisis and the veterans who had suffered under ill-treatment and discrimination found each other in a broad alliance which proved to have the potential to be a motor for change threatening the colonial status-quo.

A further case of unrest was the mutiny that broke out aboard the *Orca* bound for Barbados in September 1919. The transport ship was carrying home not only several hundred demobilized veterans including fifty prisoners from the Taranto mutiny, but also 200 black seamen and civilians repatriated in the wake of the race riots in Britain. When, despite promises to be released from custody once the ship set sail, this wasn't the case, the prisoners attempted to free themselves, assisted by other West Indians on board. During one of these attempts on 20 September 1919, a Barbadian private of the BWIR, Charles Lashley, was shot dead. He was probably buried at sea, as he is now commemorated on the Hollybrook Memorial, Southampton. And in Grenada, the transition from 1919 to 1920 saw a series of robberies and incendiary fires damaging mainly the properties of the white merchants and symbols of British authority in the capital Saint George's. The acts were vindicated by a 'T.T.T. Gang' who left typed notes on the scenes of the crime. It was generally believed the culprits were ex-servicemen influenced by T.A. Marryshow and his radical newspaper *The West Indian* as he and his supporters had been encouraging the returned soldiers to 'fight for the political, economic, social, and moral progress' of the Grenadians.

The anxiety on behalf of the officials and the discontent on behalf of a large section of the population was general throughout the British West Indies, as well as in Panama. In the latter country a strike wave was ongoing in July 1919, at the very moment the West Indian veterans were returning. At one meeting in Colón, strike leader Peter McDonald Milliard, a medical doctor born in British Guiana, addressed the veterans directly, stating: 'You men have gone over there and proved yourselves to be fighters. You have nothing for which to thank the United States or Great Britain, the people in Washington and Liverpool are murdering your race and now is the time to fight for yourselves… Since the inception of Magna Carta and the Bill of Rights, we have never received our rights'[11]. The speech, and the agitated reaction of the audience of several hundreds, was enough to alarm the British consuls in Colón and Panama City, and to see them engage in a correspondence with Chester Harding, the governor of the US held Panama Canal Zone.

Even in those colonies where eventually no disturbances took place, the authorities had been on the alert: in Barbados draconian measures were put in place to quell eventual riots, including the right to fire to kill if necessary. And when and where protests occurred, they were not necessarily voiced in a violent way. In St Kitts and Nevis – which saw no rioting in 1919 – a petition demanded full citizenship, stating that the local population was 'quite fit and capable to have a voice in the management of their own public affairs'.[12]

In this tense atmosphere, no troops from the West Indies were to take part in the grand and highly mediatized Victory Parade in the imperial capital London on 19 July 1919, a fact considered by David Olusoga as a final insult to the people of the Caribbean who had been amongst the most supportive of the war effort in 1914.[13] In 1921 the British West Indies Regiment was disbanded all together. When in 1923 the volume that included the West Indies was published in the semi-official The Empire at War series, one paragraph regretted that the regiment wasn't 'brigaded under an officer familiar with the conditions of life in the West Indies', that the men had not been 'given more chances in the firing line', that the regiment 'was divided up over the various theatres of war' and also that the increment of pay of the British soldier was initially withheld from the West Indian soldier. Regarding the last matter, which after all was one of the sources of the Taranto mutiny, the author praised the West Indian Contingent Committee to whose letter of protest it was due that 'the benefits under the Order [were] extended to the British West Indies Regiment.'[14] Hence, in this highly paternalist demonstration of history writing only the benevolence of the white ruling class was stressed. That the West Indian rank and file and NCOs had given proof a high degree of agency during the mutiny was entirely left unmentioned.

As the combination of returning soldiers and a situation of unemployment and deprivation seemed the perfect mix for continuous riots and unrest, the authorities encouraged the war veterans to emigrate. Up to the end of March 1920 free permits to Cuba were issued and thus, some 420 Barbadians and 4,000 Jamaicans or about half of the returned veterans of these islands, crossed the Caribbean Sea to the bigger island where the economy was then thriving. Among them was Eugent Clarke: 'I spent one month in Jamaica here and then I went to Cuba. In Cuba I did cane cutting. Hard work. You had to cut by the ton. They paid you a dollar a ton to cut the cane. I went to Cuba because I wanted some assistance and some money to carry on because you couldn't get a job in Jamaica'.[15] While Eugent Clarke returned to his home island after twelve years, many others remained: when 110- year-old Clifford Powell was interviewed for TV documentary Mutiny he did so partly in English and partly in Spanish in front of a Jamaican and British flag in the British West Indian Welfare Centre in Guantanamo.

For those who did not emigrate to Cuba or elsewhere, low wages or even unemployment were often in store. In Jamaica, the returning veterans, save those dishonourably discharged, were given the vote in the forthcoming elections. It was, however, a favour that only applied to the next election, not a permanent inclusion of the veterans in the franchise. As this had no effect whatsoever for their social and economic advance the veterans' claims based on their wartime experiences of discrimination would remain a central issue in politics. To the Jamaican Veterans' Association of the British West Indies Regiment that had been founded in 1919, land acquisition was a major demand. But it was not until 1924 before a settlement of free allotments for veterans was worked out. The Ex-British West Indies Regiment Association in Jamaica would remain active in the social-economic field throughout the 1920s and 1930s. In May 1933 it led a hunger march of several hundreds of veterans, including some in a wheelchair, to the Legislative Council chamber asking for immediate relief for those who had served King and Country as many veterans were in dire needs of food and housing. As a result, a new scheme of land settlement for ex-servicemen was developed. As with the earlier land acquisition programme, the quality of the land was often poor, water supplies insufficient and access to the grounds was lacking. In August 1937 the Association presented a series of demands before Governor Denham: besides preferential treatment for ex-soldiers in employment on public works and in the granting of contracts, it also addressed general labour problems as a whole. On a demonstration the day after, to bolster their demands, not less than one thousand veterans showed up.

The war had definitely changed the men, for the better or for the worse. Just like European veterans, the West Indians returned to a world which they did not entirely recognize, often traumatized and suffering from different degrees of battle neurosis. In Jamaica the asylum took in seventy-one BWIR men suffering from 'shell shock' or 'war excitement' between 1918 and 1920. In the hundred and sixth year of his life, Eugent Clarke expressed how the war had never really left him: 'But you miss the war you know. When you're in the field and there are no guns, you hear no sounds not nothing, you feel like you're out of place'.[16] For him as for so many others around the world, having been a soldier had been the defining moment of his life. Yet, the war also seemed to have made some a better person. When Emmanuel Rolle was at school with Étienne Dupuch in Nassau, he was known as a thief and the police regularly came after him. But after the war, now the devoted flag bearer of the British Legion, he was highly annoyed by the fact that another Emmanuel Rolle was constantly mentioned in the local press being charged with stealing. Each time this happened, Dupuch had to insert a notice in his newspaper stating that the Emmanuel Rolle whose name appeared in the court news was not the same person as the ex-serviceman Emmanuel Rolle. 'Wearing the King's uniform had made an honest man of him', Dupuch concludes.[17]

Chapter Five

Personal Trajectories

Veterans were not only personally inclined to become leaders, but there were also often community expectations that they would assume a leading role. A Caribbean case in point was James Barnes, a native American from British Guiana. He had served with the West India Regiment in Africa, then with the British West Indies Regiment in France and after the war he joined the Bahamas' police force in Nassau. When he left the force, Barnes settled on the remote island of Mayaguana, where practically no one had enjoyed a formal education and was literate. 'And so', he became a leader of the local community and his fellow-veteran Étienne Dupuch, to whose constituency Mayaguana belonged, had him appointed justice of the peace. And in Grenada the governor appointed in July 1919 eighteen new Justices of the Peace, eight of whom were officers and non-commissioned officers who had served overseas. One of them, Company Quartermaster William Edward Julien, declined the offer. It is believed Julien, who had won the Distinguished Conduct Medal for an act of bravery at the front, did so out of discontent with the way the veterans were being treated. Later, Julien would become a successful iron-willed businessman in Grenada. At age 72 in 1968 still remembering vividly how at the time he had been told by his English officer how his skin colour deterred him from receiving a commission.

A score of individual West Indian veterans rose to prominence after the First World War. It is an enlightening exercise to delve into their life stories to look for similarities and differences in their trajectories.

However, one thing they all shared, was that the First World War was a life-defining event.

Clennell Wilsden Wickham's sister remembered how after his return to Barbados her brother went to church in his army uniform and deliberately sat on a bench reserved for white people. The sexton came up to him and told him he couldn't sit there as it was where the white people sat. Wickham stood up and walked off, never to return to a church for the remainder of his life. Wickham was far from being the only one to become disenchanted with religion. After all, according to many, the chaplains had generally failed to put in practice the teachings of Christ. A letter that had been sent from Taranto by an anonymous BWIR sergeant is telling in this respect: 'We have no rights or privileges. We are treated neither as Christians nor as British citizens but as West Indian niggers without anybody to be interested in or look after us'.[1] None of the chaplains seems to have stood up for them, neither.

A socialist by persuasion but radicalized by his wartime experiences, Wickham became a writer and later an editor of *The Barbados Herald*, a left-leaning activist newspaper, advocating universal suffrage in the colony and successfully campaigning to end child labour in the sugar cane fields. In 1924, Wickham was co-founder of the Democratic League, Barbados' first political party, championing social and political reform in what, according to Mary Chamberlain, was 'the most economically impoverished, racially divided, socially disadvantaged, and politically conservative of the British West Indian colonies'.[2] At the same time Wickham argued for free trade among the British Caribbean territories, asking in 1928: 'Is it too much to hope, or will the West Indian colonies continue to develop each along its own lines with the certainty of getting nowhere in the end?'[3] In 1930 his newspaper was forced to close down after a libel case brought against him, causing hardship and frustration to the ex-serviceman. Wickham's Grenadian colleague T.A. Marryshow finally came to his rescue in 1934 inviting him to join as editor of the latters's *West Indian*. He died four year later, aged 43, in Grenada. Clennell Wickham is the best known but was not the only ex-BWIR man in Barbados to turn an activist. His comrade Joseph Garner was involved in both the UNIA and the Workingmen's Association, and as a consequence he was ousted by the elite-led Returned Soldier's Committee.

Due to his biography by C.L.R. James, Captain Arthur Andrew Cipriani (31 January 1875 – 18 April 1945) is probably with Manley, the best known of the West Indian First World War veterans. Cipriani was a white creole of Corsican descent and belonged to the Trinidadian elite. Until war broke out, he led an unnoticed life, yet became active in the recruitment drive, pleading for a participation of the 'coloured' segment of the population in the war effort. He served with the 5th (reserve) Battalion in Egypt and Palestine. Impressed by the war service of the West Indians, he became convinced that the West Indian people were perfectly capable of self-government. The Trinidad he returned to was an island in turmoil: retail prices had risen by 145 per cent between 1914 and 1917, and in the latter year the oil and asphalt workers had gone on strike. Troops had been called in, and five of the movement's leaders were thrown in jail. In the final year of the war, the Trinidad Workingmen's Association (TWA) which represented mainly black skilled urban workers, was revitalized. Unrest grew when the Trinidadian ex-servicemen returned home. They set up a Returned Soldiers and Sailors Council and Organization which staged public meetings at which they aired their grievances. Cipriani was soon elected president of this soldiers' and sailors' union. He vigorously attacked crown colony rule which he saw as merely an alliance between the Colonial Office and local business interests, and therefore a facade for autocracy. In 1923 Cipriani also assumed the leadership of the TWA which he would help to transform into the Trinidad Labour Party some ten years later. As an elected member of the island's Legislative Council from

1925 until his death he opposed the nominated members and their hostility to the wider public interest, being the labourers' champion, advocating minimum wages, old age pensions, abolition of child labour, and compulsory education. One of his political goals was home rule for the West Indies, something he was able to eloquently formulate: 'It is all very well and good to talk of us as "subject races". I laugh that to scorn. We are free people of the British Empire. We are entitled to the same privileges and the same form of Government and administration as our bigger sisters, the Dominions and we have got to use everything in our power.... to bring self-government and Dominion status to these beautiful Colonies'.[4] From this fragment it is clear that he mainly objected to the subordination of the 'coloured' population with whom he entirely identified, while aiming at self-rule – and not independence – within the Empire. Ever a supporter of a West Indian federation, his constant slogan was: 'Agitate, Educate, Confederate'.[5] Equally a member of the Port of Spain town council, he was several subsequent times elected mayor of the Trinidadian capital. Captain Cipriani's memory is still held in high esteem in Trinidad, and he has a statue in downtown Port of Spain, a city with otherwise very few monuments to individuals.

Still in Trinidad, in the late 1930s, Captain Cipriani's star was eclipsed by that of Grenadian-born Tubal Uriah Buzz Butler (21 January 1897–20 February 1977). Butler who had been schooled until age thirteen only, had served as a private in the British West Indies Regiment, and his low regimental number might be an indication that he was among the very first to join up. Returning to Grenada at the age of 21, he joined the Grenada Representative Government Movement and the Grenada Union of Returned Soldiers, and he became associated with Marcus Garvey's UNIA. It was rumoured he had a stake in the series of arsons committed by the 'T.T.T.Gang' in the capital of St George's in late 1919–early 1920. Sometime later, Butler moved to Trinidad. There, he would rise to prominence in

1935 by leading the unemployed in a hunger march from the oilfields to Port of Spain. A Spiritual Baptist preacher, his teaching has been described as an odd mixture of the Bible and Marxism. Originally a staunch follower of Captain Cipriani, Butler was expelled from the Trinidad Labour Party in 1936 for his extremist tendencies, going on to establish the British Empire Workers' and Citizens' Home Rule Party. Its very name was an indication of Butler's conviction: like Cipriani he was highly critical of the existing colonial regime while remaining attached to the British connection. In 1937 he headed a general strike which originated among the mainly black oil workers in the southern Trinidadian city of Fyzabad, and whose main issues were working conditions, higher wages, racism, and a reform of the political system. Before order was restored fourteen were killed, fifty-nine wounded, and hundreds arrested. An arrest warrant for Butler was issued and he went into hiding. Despite a promised safe passage to testify at a commission of enquiry into the events, Butler was arrested when he emerged, and subsequently imprisoned from September 1937 to May 1939. Just some months later, on the outbreak of the Second World War, he was re-arrested as he was considered a threat to one of the British Empire's main supplies of petroleum and he remained detained for the remainder of the war. After his release from prison, he re-entered politics with the Butler Home Rule Party – later the Butler Party, whose popularity after initial success, declined with every election. Butler, the first African Caribbean leader to emerge in Trinidad, is considered the founding father of the Oilfields Workers' Trade Union (OWTU) and the Trinidadian labour movement and he is honoured with a statue in Fyzabad. He was awarded the Trinity Cross, the nation's highest honour, in 1970.

Both from Chaplain Horner's remarks on the importance of music to the West Indian rank and file and of the West Indian Contingent Committee's effort to provide a band for each of the battalions, it can be reckoned that many fine musicians were to be found among the BWIR men. Probably the finest of them was Sam Manning (c. 1898–1960) from Trinidad who had originally joined up with the Middlesex Regiment before being transferred to the BWIR. This raises the question how common the practice was to transfer 'coloured' West Indians who had joined regular British regiments to the BWIR after the latter was formed. It has been stated that 'most blacks who had previously succeeded in enlisting in regular units of the British Army were forcibly transferred to the BWIR, whether they were West Indian or not'.[6] This certainly fitted in with British official policy – an example being the Māori in the New Zealand infantry who were 'pushed' to join the New Zealand (Māori) Pioneer Battalion once this was established – yet Manning is the only person we know of such a transfer in the case of West Indians. Brothers Roy and Norman Manley, on whom I focus later in this chapter, always stayed with their regular British unit, even though they were 'coloured' and suffered hardship as a result. Otherwise, little is known on his military career, but Manning would go on to become an icon of West Indian culture in New York, London, and in other places. He was not only a pioneering black recording artist, one of the world's finest Calypsonians, and an actor, but also the companion of Marcus Garvey's ex-wife and co-founder of the UNIA, Amy Ashwood Garvey. In this companionship of a BWIR veteran and a well-known Pan-Africanist spokesperson one could see an almost literal marriage of the West Indian war experience with political activism.

In his own words Sir Étienne Dupuch (16 Feb 1898–23 Aug 1991) from the Bahamas was a changed man 'after having seen the peoples of Europe wallowing in a cesspit of human degradation'. He came to realize that the Colonial Office was 'completely out of touch with the dark races in her global possessions, and only had an ear for the "Old Guard" ruling groups in the colonies'. Back in Nassau in 1919, aged just 20, he was initially a bitter man swearing never again to lift a finger for King and Country, or for anything that did not belong to his own sphere. Yet, after a while he recalled the words of that Sikh on the deck of the ship which brought them to France upon being treated ill by a brutal and impolite Englishman that it was not for these that the war was fought but for the grand British ideal. And this ideal meant to him 'the rule of law without which freedom dies aborning'.[7] Though at first reluctant, this insight urged him to take over the newspaper his father had founded in 1903. *The Tribune* was the first newspaper in the Bahamas that represented all opinions in the colony, including those of the 'coloured' population, voiceless until then. The newspaper's office also served as the meeting place for returned soldiers in need of a friend. Dupuch and his *Tribune* opposed Nassau's ruling white élite and was thus unpopular with the establishment, and during the Second World War he heavily criticized the Duke of Windsor, then governor of the Bahamas, for his racist attitudes. Yet, later he also spoke out against the leftist and populist Progressive Liberal Party (PLP) believing the Bahamas should follow a middle way in resolving political differences between blacks and whites. Due to his outspoken opinions, his newspaper office was often the scene of public protests. A long-standing member of the House of Assembly, Dupuch is seen as the principal author of the first comprehensive anti-discrimination legislation in the Bahamas, which outlawed racial segregation and discrimination in 1956. It was the achievement he was most proud of and which he directly related to his wartime experiences. Being appointed a Member of the Order of the British Empire (OBE) in 1948, he was knighted by Elisabeth II in 1964, In later life he became oddly out of fashion in the Bahamas as he advocated a strong loyalty to Britain and was exceptionally critical of the pursuit of independence. In 1972, one year before the latter's realization, he even went into voluntary exile for some time in Coral Gables, near Miami, dissatisfied with the politics of the ruling PLP in his country. In 1991, this remarkable man died in a remarkable way when he caught fire while destroying an ants' nest in his garden. To this day, Dupuch is known as the longest serving newspaper editor ever.

Already during the war Corporal Samuel A. Haynes (1899–1971) rose to prominence. In his song 'The Die-Hards Triumph' which was published in the British Honduras' newspaper, *The Clarion*, on 12 April 1917, he spoke up for the black soldiers, warning those at home that when returned they would collect their 'Military Pay' to live in comfort. Little more than two years later, he would live up to his promise, when he emerged as one of the leaders of the returned servicemen during the Belize riots of July 1919. In his testimony before the Commission of Inquiry into the disturbances, Haynes explicitly referred to the discriminatory circumstances he had encountered while on service, how they had been transported in a dirty ship hold and in cattle trucks, and how the West Indians had to live through the Mesopotamian winter in leaking huts without any flooring, while the British soldiers were lodged in huts equipped with electric lights, floorboards, and stoves. As secretary of the Contingent Committee, he tried in May 1920 without success to obtain the release from prison of the veterans who had been arrested after the riots. Yet, he played a more important role as the leader of Garvey's UNIA in British Honduras where he was assisted by Benjamin Adderley, another BWIR veteran. Later he was asked by Garvey to move to the United States, where he practically became his right-hand man. Haynes served the UNIA in Pittsburgh, Baltimore, Philadelphia, North and South Carolina, and Delaware. A regular contributor to the UNIA's organ *Negro World*, Haynes assumed de facto leadership of the organization when Garvey returned to his native Jamaica in 1934. Two years later, he would publicly break with the old leader when the latter refused to change his negative attitude towards the Ethiopian emperor Haile Selassie. By then the glory days of the UNIA were definitely over, something Haynes acknowledged. He continued to work for a number of newspapers while leading the

Harlem-based Pan-Africanist journal, *The African*, never relenting his convictions. 'The civilisation fostered by British imperialism is damned and doomed', he predicted in 1946.[8] Despite his remarkable career, Haynes is nowadays mainly remembered as the author of the 1925 song 'Land of the Gods' that in 1981, ten years after his death, as 'Land of the Free' became the national anthem of his newly independent fatherland, Belize, former British Honduras.

Though Norman Manley (4 July 1893–2 September 1969) did not serve in the British West Indies Regiment, his inclusion in a book which focuses on the West Indian experience of the Western Front is a must. As probably the best known Caribbean veteran of the First World War, his war experiences show similarities with many who served in the BWIR. Born in 1893 to a well-off Jamaican family – his father was a white businessman and his mother half-Irish – the slightly 'coloured' Manley was reading law at Oxford's Jesus College when war broke out. Despite having attended a good public school, his younger brother Douglas Roy, known as Roy, was initially refused in an Officers Training Corps because of his skin colour. Subsequently, in September 1915 the two brothers signed up together in the Royal Field Artillery, doing so in working class Deptford where non-white men were more easily accepted by locals and army officials alike. When four months later he went overseas, Norman Manley did so as a corporal. Yet, his rank proved to be a disadvantage as the ordinary gunners 'disliked taking orders from a coloured NCO and their attitude was mild by comparison with that of my fellow NCO's... They were more spiteful and later conspired to get me into trouble'.[9] When this indeed happened, he managed to escape court martial through a deal with his sympathetic commanding officer: Manley was transferred with his brother to "D" Battery of the 174th Brigade of the RFA and – on his own proposal – reverted to the rank of gunner. In the run-up to the Third Battle of Ypres, his brother Roy was killed in action on 26 July 1917, 21 years old, now commemorated in Poperinghe New Military Cemetery, grave II.E.41. Norman wasn't near him when his brother was struck by a small part of shell casing, but helped bury him the next day. Some months later, still during the Third Battle of Ypres, Manley was awarded the Military Medal for conspicuous bravery in the field. Without his brother, he felt more alone as ever and he attributed this to his skin colour. After the war, returning to Oxford, Manley faced problems adapting to civil life, maybe suffering from war neurosis, finally graduating in 1921 and marrying his cousin and love for some years, the English artist Edna Swithenbank. After his return to Jamaica, he became the leading lawyer of the island and in 1938 he founded the People's National party, championing universal suffrage and self-government. The former would be granted in 1944, the latter gradually culminated in Jamaica's independence in 1962. Universal suffrage was for Manley a way to establish national unity in Jamaica. Following Garveyist thought, he broke away from the imperial version of history and replaced it with a concept of history as a search for origins that were both Jamaican and ennobling. Manley eventually became Chief Minister of Jamaica from 1955 to 1959 and Premier from 1959–1962. He strongly advocated to join the short-lived West Indies Federation in 1958 believing it would be a vehicle to obtain self-government. After a referendum decided to leave the federation, he chaired the committee that prepared a new constitution and negotiated independence for Jamaica. Shortly after his death in 1969, he was given the title of National Hero, one of seven Jamaicans to whom the title was conferred. According to his granddaughter Rachel, throughout his life Norman Manley always wore a black tie in memory of his beloved brother with whom he had joined the army in England but who never returned.[10]

Another remarkable First World War veteran in Jamaica, much lesser known in Europe, is Sergeant William Wellington Wellwood Grant. Grant (1894–1977) had served in the 11th Battalion of the

BWIR. As so many he couldn't find work upon his return after the war, and he emigrated to New York. While working in a restaurant, he became heavily involved in the UNIA of his fellow Jamaican Marcus Garvey. Besides doing voluntary work as a cook in Harlem's Liberty Hall and learning African History, William Grant mainly trained the movement's security forces, a job which must have particularly suited him as an ex-NCO in the British Army. Garvey's Royal African Guard were elegantly attired in magnificent uniforms and their appearance during parades and meetings other events had to instil pride in the black community. Grant was far from the only BWIR veteran to become involved in Garvey's militia: his Bahamian peer James B. Nimmons, for instance, trained the Miami unit. When Grant returned to Jamaica in 1934, he worked as a street food vendor. As he was struck by the poverty he encountered on the island and as a trained Garveyite activist, he now dedicated his free time to the empowerment of the poor. This Grant mainly did as a soap box orator, making speeches to sometimes large crowds after church meetings. The sergeant discussed world affairs, for instance showing himself furious when Mussolini invaded Ethiopia in late 1935. When addressing a crowd, Grant always wore one of his many uniforms, his two war medals prominently pinned on his chest. This he did not solely for decorum. The medals made clear to his followers and his opponents that it was his war service and his capacity as a veteran that entitled him to lead the masses and to raise his voice in public. Over time, the subject of William Grant's speeches shifted from African history to labour issues, and he invited the emerging labour leader (and Norman Manley's cousin and later bitter rival) Alexander Bustamante to share his stage. Bustamante (1884–1977) would eventually become the first prime minister of independent Jamaica. On 2 May 1938 Sergeant Grant lead a crowd of some 3000 supporters to the offices of *The Jamaica Standard* to ask support and sympathy from the editor and to expose poverty and bad payment of the labourers, while one day later he led a smaller

A recruiting meeting in Kingston Jamaica, 1914–15. Published in Cundall F, *Jamaica's Part in the Great War*. (London: West India Committee, 1925)

Recruits from British Honduras leaving Belize. (*Belize Archives and Records Service*)

Departure of a contingent for the BWIR from Belize, British Honduras. (*Belize Archives and Records Service*)

Bahamian recruiting poster for the British West Indies Regiment.

The badge of the British West Indies Regiment, designed by the West Indian Contingent Committee. A clear, dignified but also neutral design, it affirmed a single West Indian identity.

Three photographs of a camp of the British West Indies Regiment, somewhere in Belgium, photographed by Belgian soldier Jérôme Renneboog. (*Town archives Aalst, G. Renneboog collection*)

Eugène Burnand (1850–1921): Cephus Johnson, from Jamaica. Published as a portrait of "Cafés Johnson" in *Les Alliés Dans La Guerre Des Nations* (Paris: Crété, 1922)

West Indian soldiers photographed in Poperinghe, Flanders, 1917 (*In Flanders Fields Museum, Ypres*)

A West Indian soldier posing with early battlefield tourists in the ruins Ypres, 1919. (*Collection Westflandrica, Kortrijk*)

Gwalia Cemetery, Poperinghe, Belgium. Six graves belong to the West Indian casualties of the bombardment of 29 July 1917 so vividly described by Bahamian Etienne Dupuch in his memoirs. They include that of the ill-fated sergeant Sparkman, a Florida man who had settled in the Bahamas. (*Author's photograph*)

The headstone of the 20 year old Jamaican jew Alan Florizel Sampson who served in the 4th battalion BWIR, and succombed to a war related sickness on 5 February 1917 in Wimereux, France. (*Author's photograph*)

The headstone of Ernest Brooks, from Sea View Farm, Antigua, on Dozinghem Cemetery, West-Vleteren, Belgium. (*Photo: Rudi Wille*)

Seventeen year old Herbert Morris was executed on 20 September 1917. He is buried in Poperinghe New Military Cemetery in Belgium, coincidentally also the burial place of fellow-Jamaican Roy Manley, brother of future Prime Minister Norman Manley. (*Photo: Rudi Wille*)

In 1919, the year West Indians in the United Kingdom became victims of racial prejudice and violence, this cartoon by Chas Grave was published in Punch. In it, the men of the British West Indies Regiment are stereotyped as loafing stragglers.

No fanfare on the return of the last BWIR contingent in Jamaica, 1919. Published in Cundall F, *Jamaica's Part in the Great War*. (London: West India Committee, 1925)

Etienne Dupuch was 17 years old when he joined the fifth Bahamas war contingent. Before leaving, he had his photograph taken, wearing the uniform of the local militia and surrounded by family members. Published in his memoirs *A Salute to Friend & Foe*. (Nassau: The Tribune, 1982)

Sergeant William Wellington Wellwood Grant joined Marcus Garvey's Universal Negro Improvement Association in 1920s New York. After his return to Jamaica he became one of the country's leading trade unionists and labour activists. In his honour Victoria Park in Jamaica's capital Kingston was renamed St. William Grant Park. (*National Library of Jamaica*)

Jamaican brothers Norman (standing) and Roy Manley served in the Royal Field Artillery but also suffered due to their skin colour. Roy got killed in Flanders, while Norman became one of Jamaica's greatest statesmen. (*Courtesy of the Manley family*)

The War Memorial in Castries, St Lucia (detail). (*Photo: Mike Reys*)

Armistice Day at the War Memorial in Kingston, Jamaica. (*Photo: Derrian Barrant*)

The Roll of Honour on the Dominica War Memorial in Roseau.

The names of the British West Indies Regiment on the Menin Gate Memorial to the Missing, Ypres, Belgium. (*Author's photograph*)

group of some 500 shouting 'down with Imperialism', accompanying reporters and photographers to see the poor living conditions in a very deprived area of Kingston known as the Dunghill or 'Dungle'. When, later that month, a strike of wharf workers broke out, he was asked by the stevedores to act as their leader. Despite his unmistakable political skills, the strikers might have believed his status as an ex-soldier would make the authorities more indulgent towards their demands. This, however, was not the case and after heavy riots and the occupation of an official building Grant was arrested on 23 May 1938 along with Bustamante. Following the promulgation of a Riot Act, British troops were called in, the occupation was forcibly ended, and the crowd dispersed – these events were eventually the trigger for Norman Manley to enter politics. Though obtaining a pay rise, the striking wharf workers continued their struggle until Bustamante and Grant were released from prison. Shortly after their release, in June 1938, both men would formally establish a trade union. Bustamante and Grant later became at odds with each other when the latter fully supported Manley in his movement for self-government. Grant was often involved in street fights which he more and more lost, eventually leading to his withdrawal from public life. Gradually returned to a state of near poverty, he received official recognition towards the end of his life, always remaining not only a convinced follower of Garvey but also a proud veteran: until his death he wore the uniform of UNIA's paramilitary Tiger Division with the British War Medal and Victory Medal he had earned during the First World War pinned on his chest. When he died, he was given a state funeral and shortly after Victoria Park in Kingston was renamed St William Grant Park.

This survey of veterans-turned-activists makes clear that though their ex-commander Lieutenant Colonel Wood-Hill had in 1921 expressed the wish that military discipline had made the West Indians 'immune to political radicalisation'[11] rather the inverse seems to have been the case. While some returning veterans did eventually become noted pillars of society – Sir Étienne Dupuch in the Bahamas proves the point – many others were precisely radicalized through their war experience and not seldom choose a more confrontational way to obtain their goals. It was particularly in the social upheavals that struck the Caribbean in the mid-1930s that unrewarded contributions of the West Indian war effort were invoked, and the former soldiers were called to play their role. As these individual trajectories made clear, West Indian activism as expressed by the BWIR veterans could be insular nationalist (towards the advancement of the individual colony) or federal nationalist (towards a federation of the West Indies), racial (towards the advancement of the black segment of the population), or transracial (towards creole multiculturalism).

Chapter Six

West Indian Veterans between Nationalism and Pan-Africanism

Apart from the direct political impact some of the veterans exercised in the British West Indies, there was equally an important indirect influence on the activist upsurge in the region at large between the wars. The men who had made up the British West Indies Regiment had come from all parts of the British Caribbean, all had family and friends, who would learn about the racism and discrimination they had suffered. Their experiences and opinions were equally propagated by the radical press. Thus, their anger and indignation trickled down to the general population. The servicemen had been politically radicalized by their war experiences and with them their home societies radicalized.

The racial discrimination the men from the British West Indies Regiment had experienced, had certainly entrenched a sense of racial consciousness into their emerging West Indian groupness. The war had lifted them out of the insularity of their own island or mainland colonies, and had flung them in a context where they stood out as West Indians and as black troops, suffering the same treatment as other non-white troops of the British Empire. Their temporary migration during the First World War had enhanced the West Indians' identification with both a national (that of the colony) and a transnational entity (that of the West Indies) and reinforced Black cultural consciousness. Therefore, we see at the same time a creole multiracial nationalism (e.g. Cipriani, Manley), focused on either the island or the broader region, with little or no attention to matters of skin colour, and a more racialized nationalism which strongly identified with the African character (e.g. Haynes, Grant).

The quest for political reform which had been initiated before the war, was reinvigorated after 1919, representative government and an enlargement of the base of franchise being the main demands. Yet now the challenge to crown colony rule was no longer being undertaken only within the individual territories but had also become a subject of political activity on a regional basis in the British West Indies. Apart from Barbados and the Bahamas, crown colony rule still prevailed everywhere. Some leaders, such as T.A. Marryshow in Grenada, Captain Cipriani in Trinidad, and Cecil Rawle in Dominica also advocated a unification of the West Indies, but this was far from the rule. In Grenada in 1917 a Representative Government Association had been founded of which Buz Butler would become a member, while similar organizations also saw the light in other colonies. Not least so in Jamaica where the veterans were struggling to get recognition for their wartime sacrifices. The Jamaica League which included some ex-servicemen increasingly promoted nationalist activities. The organization had some common ground with the British West Indies Regiment Association, such as advocating the establishment of co-operative stores. When in July 1919, Trinidadian Felix E.M. Hercules, the aforementioned secretary-general of the London-based Society of Peoples of African Origin, toured Jamaica after having campaigned against the racial attacks in Britain, he shared the floor with members of the Jamaica League. Not unlike Garvey, for Hercules, racial unity, pride, and consciousness were essential to any campaign for social and political advancement of African Caribbeans. This appealed heavily to the enhanced political, including racial, consciousness of the returned BWIR men. Yet, Hercules also drew on the veterans' example when he emphasized their fate of unemployment and emigration after having loyally served. Part of Hercules' proposals was a franchise enlarged to encompass all educated men, as a first step towards self-government. Still in Jamaica, trade Unionist Alfred Mends likewise pleaded for the extension of franchise within the framework of the Empire. Mends' rhetoric tied in with that of the veterans as he too argued that military service had entitled them to full citizenship.

Because of the increasingly vocal protests, London sent the Parliamentary Under-Secretary of State for the Colonies to the West Indies. Edward Wood, soon to become Viceroy of India as baron Irwin before proceeding his political career as Lord Halifax, understood that the demands for at least a level of representative government could no longer be denied but the recommendations he made to, and which were accepted by, the Colonial Office were too minor concessions in the eyes of West Indian public opinion. Nowhere were truly representative parliaments to be introduced and overall still less than three per cent of the population would be qualified to vote. It was also to prove a slow process. Only in 1925 were elected members added to the legislatures of Trinidad, Grenada, St Vincent, and St Lucia. Four of the five Leeward Islands presidencies and British Honduras even had to wait until 1936 before a portion of their legislature was chosen by the public. In British Guiana, where the Dutch-influenced constitution was replaced with a crown colony constitution in 1928, the reforms were even considered a regression. In Jamaica where all BWIR veterans had been entitled to vote in the first elections after the war and only in that one, property qualifications equally remained de rigueur. Here, in December 1944 the first elections of members to the House of Representatives were held with full adult suffrage. Yet, this concerned only one of the two chambers of the legislature, the members of the Legislative Council still being appointed. The reforms had given the British Caribbean population no opportunity to experience full political responsibility and the result was that when independence was achieved the only type of government which the British West Indies had known was authoritarian.

Both Cary Fraser and Nigel Bolland saw three reasons for the increased race and class consciousness in the British West Indies after the First World War: economic hardship and government oppression; the influence of Garveyism; and the return of demobilized soldiers of the BWIR who were bitter about the discrimination they had encountered.[1] The three phenomena are heavily intertwined and it is clear that all over the Caribbean and in the Caribbean diaspora veterans were prepared to take up a leading role in labour movements and Garveyite organizations. And it was these that would in turn lead the struggle for self-government and eventual independence. For when the Great Depression caused widespread unemployment and acute hardship, there were in most territories no democratically established channels to give vent to popular anger. The result was widespread unrest and a series of sometimes bloody disturbances, from 1933 in succession in Trinidad, in British Honduras, in St Kitts, again in Trinidad, then in Jamaica, St Lucia, British Guiana, Barbados, and St Vincent. It is from this civil strife, in which veterans played a role, that established West Indian nationalism and the demand for autonomy and independence was born, as trade unions, reform leagues, and other organizations morphed into political parties. In Britain, these organizations found an advocate in the League of Coloured Peoples (1931 –), led by Dr. Harold Moody, brother-in-law to Norman Manley, who actively campaigned for political and social-economic reforms in the British West Indian territories.

After the 1930s disturbances, the British government formed a commission of inquiry in 1938, led by the former Conservative MP, and South African War and First World War veteran, Lord Moyne, and hence known as the Moyne Commission. Its report, that was only published in 1945, confirmed the crushing poverty and injustice in the British Caribbean possessions and suggested reforms including more financial assistance from the British Treasury, slum clearance, a greater role for labour unions, self-government, and a Caribbean federation. It thus officially confirmed many of the demands BWIR veterans had taken to their heart.

Meanwhile the Second World War had been fought. Despite all the agitation of the interwar years and the contested legacy of the British West Indies Regiment, many young African Caribbeans had once again rallied around the flag. This time, however, the British authorities were to exercise greater discretion in how the West Indian soldiers were treated: they were allowed to join regular British regiments and were no longer relegated to 'mere' labour battalions. Many joined the Royal Air Force, some of whom served as officers in flying operations. In April 1944 a Caribbean Regiment of 4,000 volunteers was formed which trained in the USA, proceeded overseas in July 1944, and served in North Africa, Italy, Egypt, and Palestine before being disbanded in 1946.

While the influence of West Indian veterans and their war experience, both direct and indirect, in the move towards full citizenship and independence of the British Caribbean has been sufficiently demonstrated, it was equally of importance in the emergence and development of Black nationalism and Pan-Africanism. While nationalism focuses on the advancement of the individual colonies, Black nationalism and Pan-Africanism transcend national boundaries and focus on racial unity. Black nationalism thus turns towards a racial definition of national identity, stressing unity among Africans and freedom from European hegemony. While historian Imanuel Geiss[2] stressed it was difficult or perhaps even impossible to provide a clear definition of Pan-Africanism, Rodney Worrell defines it as 'a movement and an ideology of African peoples globally that is concerned with the social, political, economic, and psychological upliftment, as well as the protection of Africa and African peoples worldwide' and describes it as the highest stage of Black nationalism.[3] Michelle Stephens on the other hand coined the term Black *trans*nationalism to describe the same phenomenon.[4]

The man who politically vindicated the military sacrifices made by people of African descent during the First World War best and loudest was Marcus Garvey, the founder and leader of the Universal Negro Improvement Association (UNIA). With maybe up to four million members at its height in the early 1920s, this was the largest and most powerful Black nationalist organization that has ever existed, with chapters in African communities all over the world, as well as in the 'mother continent'. Its legacy, especially in the United States, endures to this day. Like so many minority leaders throughout the British Empire, in 1914, Garvey had believed that the support and blood sacrifice of African Caribbeans would be duly rewarded. During the war his newspaper *Negro World* was read by BWIR men posted overseas and according to the War Office Garvey corresponded with West Indian soldiers. Disappointed in his belief that the British Empire would reward the African Caribbean war effort with equal opportunities and citizenship, and now operating from Harlem, from 1919 onwards, he evoked the sacrifices made by black soldiers in the British Empire, in the French Empire, and in the United States of America for the cause of black unity and the redemption of an African homeland. In a speech at Carnegie Hall in the summer of 1919 Garvey stated:

> They took two million black men from America, from the West Indies, and Africa, to fight for this farcical democracy they told us about; and now we are after winning the fight, winning the battle, we realize that we are without democracy; and we come before the world, therefore, as the Universal Improvement Association, to demand our portion of democracy.[5]

Garvey effectively challenged the Imperial government to prove that the war had indeed been fought for freedom and democracy by ending white minority rule and granting full citizenship to all in the West Indies. He also supported other subordinate groups throughout the Empire and in other allied polities who now claimed sovereignty. One of his aims was to establish a 'Dominion of Negroes' in Africa.

In March 1921 Garvey toured Cuba and Jamaica where he spoke to thousands of British West Indian labourers, including many veterans, addressing them not as 'British born subjects' but as 'citizens of Africa'. He especially called on the ex-soldiers to agitate for 'African liberation'. The attractive power Garvey seemed to have had on black veterans was enhanced by his use of military-style uniforms, regalia, titles, and rituals which had to invoke pride in the wearer. When on 10 October 1921 BWIR veterans celebrated Cuba's Independence Day, they did so parading in military regalia of the UNIA's African Legion. And in the previous chapter I have already sketched how former BWIR men such as Samuel Haynes and St William Grant played an important role in Garvey's organization. Especially when Mussolini's troops threatened to invade Ethiopia in the mid 1930s, feelings ran high among the West Indian veterans, and some had letters published in the press calling to enlist in the Ethiopian army. The UNIA duly petitioned King George V to suspend the 1870 Foreign Enlistment Act that forbade British subjects to fight against a state that was not formally at war with Britain.

Garvey was without doubt the most important West Indian activist who was based in the United States, but there were many more. According to Winston James, British Caribbean migrants to the States shared a number of characteristics that disposed them towards radical politics: a majority consciousness; a political and organizational experience; an experience of travel and migration; a lesser attachment to the Christian faiths and its churches; a protected status as British subjects; and especially educational and cultural attainments beyond the reach of African Americans.[6] And few could boast of more of these criteria than the BWIR veterans. Moreover, they had the prestige attached to the status of veteran, and had experienced racial discrimination during their service. Little wonder then that many West Indian ex-servicemen were to be found among the most radical black migrants in the States, where they would often side with equally radicalized black US ex-servicemen. Some, like Samuel Haynes, had even travelled to the United States precisely because they had been radicalized. Apart from Haynes and the aforementioned Sergeant Grant, there were other black British Caribbean ex-servicemen who rose to prominence in the USA, such as Arnold Ford from Barbados. Author of the popular 'Universal Ethiopian Anthem' of the UNIA and the musical director of the UNIA's Liberty Hall in Harlem, Ford became the leader of New York's black Jews and migrated to Ethiopia in the early 1930s, dying there in 1935. The existence of a British West Indian World War Veterans' Association in New York in the 1920s is proof to their considerable number in that city. As a 'sustained project of diasporic identity building'[7], Garveyism gave the war experiences of the West Indian veterans a sense which echoed far beyond Garvey's native Jamaica, even far beyond the British West Indies and throughout the African diaspora.

Conclusion

The creation of the British West Indies Regiment in 1915 had been a direct result of the display of self-awareness on behalf of a portion of the 'coloured' and black West Indian population who demanded the possibility of enlisting. For these men, to take the King's shilling was to demonstrate their Britishness, their allegiance to King and Empire, and their self-consciousness as British subjects. It was a source of pride. This was even more so as these West Indians in no way considered themselves auxiliaries: the BWIR was formed and trained as an infantry regiment, and the men of the first contingents were trained soldiers, and no mere labourers. Moreover, many recruits, certainly in these first contingents, were educated people who read newspapers, who wrote home, who reflected on their situation, who debated, and who were ready to take action when unjustly treated.

Yet, the attitudes of the authorities vacillated between regarding the BWIR members as full-fledged infantrymen and 'native labourers', but certainly on the Western front it tended towards the latter. The idea of having black men in British uniform fighting other white men, even if these white men were the enemy, was abhorrent to the powers that be. And so, while they saw themselves first and foremost as soldiers, proud and full of self-esteem, the servicemen of the British West Indies Regiment were used as navvies. This subordinated role, attributed by others once they were overseas, was entirely due to the colour of their skin. The racial discrimination to which they had been subjected in a context in which they were waging life and limb for the nation was obviously experienced as a great injustice by the men from the Caribbean. Not only did they act when they felt the unfairness was too great, but they also internalized these feelings. What they experienced during the Great War would ultimately shape them into who they would become in later life.

In the colonial world, the Great War and its horrors had swept away the aura of the superiority of Europe's civilization and of the idea of white supremacy. In the words of Bahamian Dupuch, he had seen 'the peoples of Europe wallowing in a cesspit of human degradation'. Combined with the way the black soldiers of the BWIR had been treated during the war, one of the consequences was that the justification of colonial rule in the territories of the West Indies no longer went unchallenged. As elsewhere in the world, the final period of the war and the immediate post-war period saw an intense phase of anticolonial mobilization, the 'first signs of a fundamental legitimation crisis in colonial rule to surface, a crisis that erupted openly in the decades to follow.'[1] During this stepping stone towards decolonization, intellectual critique and social mobilization went hand in hand, aiming at the removal of abuses and discriminatory structures, and the labour struggle was an important arena for anticolonial activities. It is something we clearly see in the British territories in the Caribbean, just as we see it in other places in the British and French empires.

Most men in the Caribbean demobilized from war service probably never took part in any overt political activity. Like many other First World War veterans around the world, their primary concern was the daily struggle for economic survival. After the turbulent war years they had experienced, many longed only for a quiet life. And no doubt, as we see with (East) Indian and French African veterans, some used their status as veterans to enter government service, thus becoming pillars of the colonial administration. However, rarely is it so evident as in the British West Indies that veterans of the past war took up leading roles in the movement that contested the colonial status-quo:

a significant number of West Indian veterans became protagonists in the emerging movement for self-government, universal suffrage and social justice that would ultimately lead to the independence of almost all the British colonies in the Caribbean while many others got engaged in the international phenomena of Black nationalism and Pan-Africanism, stressing unity among Africans and striving towards freedom from European hegemony. But whatever path they chose, all had been marked by their experiences in the First World War.

> Lads of the West, with duty done, soon shall we parted be
> To different land, perhaps no more each other's face to see,
> But still as comrades of the war our efforts we'll unite
> To sweep injustice from our land, its social wrongs to right.
> Then go on conquering – lift your lives above each trivial thing
> To which the meaner breeds of earth so desperately, cling;
> And Heaven grant you strength to fight the battle for your race,
> To fight and conquer, making earth for man a happier place.

Henry B. Monteith, Acting Warrant Officer Class 2, British West Indies Regiment, *Jamaica Times*, 28 June 1919.[2]

Appendix 1

Composition and Service of the British West Indies Regiment

1st (Infantry)	June 1915	Egypt and Palestine
2nd (Infantry)	January 1916	Egypt and Palestine
3rd (Infantry)	January 1916	Egypt, France and Flanders as from Aug/Sep 1916
4th (Infantry)	May 1916	Egypt, France and Flanders as from Aug/Sep 1916
5th (Reserve)	August 1916	reserve, in Egypt
6th (Service)	March 1917	France and Flanders
7th (Service)	March 1917	France and Flanders
8th (Service)	July 1917	France and Flanders, Italy
9th (Service)	July 1917	France and Flanders, Italy (disbanded Jan 1919)
10th (Service)	August 1917	France and Flanders, Italy
11th (Service)	October 1917	Italy
12th (Service)	?/1917	Italy

The *approximate* total strength of the British West Indies Regiment, each colony's *approximate* share in the strength of the BWIR (and that number in relation to the colony's population)[1]

Total: 397 officers + 15,204 Other Ranks = 15,601

Jamaica (including the Turks and Caicos Islands, the Cayman Islands, and many West Indians residing abroad, e.g. in Panama): 10,280 or 66% (1.1% of the population)

Trinidad (including Tobago): ca 1,480 or 9.5% (0.43% of the population)

Barbados: 831 or 5.3% (0.47% of the population)

British Guiana: 700 or 4.5% (0.23% of the population)

British Honduras: 533 or 3.5% (1.33% of the population)

Grenada: 445 or 2.9% (0.67% of the population)

Bahamas: 441* or 2.9% (0.7 % of the population)

St Lucia: 359 or 2.3% (0.72% of the population)

St Vincent: 305** or 2% (0.66% of the population)

Leeward Islands (Anguilla, Antigua, Barbuda, British Virgin Islands, Dominica, Montserrat, Nevis, and St Kitts: 229 or 1.5% (0.18% of the population)

---

* 486 according to Lucas C P, *The Empire at War*. Vol. 2. (Oxford: Oxford University Press, 1921), p. 427. The same source notes that 50 Bahamian labourers joined from Panama.

** 538 according to *Ibid.*, p. 398.

Appendix 2

Writing the History of the British West Indies Regiment

According to B.W. Higman in the *Oxford History of the British Empire*, the historiography of the West Indies has been a persistently underdeveloped field and this despite the long British colonial experience in the Caribbean.[1] Twentieth century histories of the British Empire have often slighted the West Indies, while race and racism have always been important themes in the historiography of the territories. This also counts for the West Indies in the First World War: the field is certainly underdeveloped, with only two dedicated monographs, yet the issue of colour is quintessential in understanding the West Indian experience of the war. The situation is even more astonishing when we take into account that historical overviews such as *The Caribbean. A History of the Region and Its Peoples*, published in 2011, do stress the importance of the West Indian war experience for its post-First World War developments.

While during and immediately after the war occasional letters from BWIR members and reports on their doings were published in the West Indian press, no diaries, stories, or memoirs – either by officers or by the rank and file – were published in separate print, the sole exception being the accounts by two chaplains. The first one, already published in 1917 by Jamaican-born J. Ramson who had accompanied the 6th Battalion on its voyage to France, was rather brief. More of interest are the sketches from Europe which his colleague Alfred Egbert Horner had published serially in the *Nassau Tribune* and which were published in their entirety in 1919. Rev Alfred Horner who had accompanied a Bahamas contingent and served in the 6th and 9th battalions, wanted to highlight for a domestic public the works of those he persistently calls 'our boys'. Everything he considered nasty and unpleasant has largely been omitted: hence one will not find anything on the execution of one of the 'boys' from his battalion in September 1917 nor on the mutiny in Taranto in December 1919.

Probably due to the unrest provoked by the return of the black servicemen, little if nothing was published on the men's war experiences war during the 1920s. What was published on the West Indies in the war were more general, sanitized overviews and reports such as Frank Cundall's *Jamaica's part in the Great War* or the volume containing the contributions on the West Indies in Charles Lucas' multi-volume semi-official *The Empire at War.*

Between 1929 and 1931 the black Trinidadian activist journalist and historian C.L.R. James wrote *The Life of Captain Cipriani: An Account of British Government in the West Indies* in which a chapter was devoted to the role of the British West Indies Regiment. Based on lengthy interviews he had with Cipriani, a white elite Creole, James demonstrated how the war experiences had politicized the captain and led him to lead the Trinidad Workingmen's Association against the local colonial elite, yet there is not so much on the history of the BWIR itself and his story focuses mainly on Trinidad and Cipriani's struggle. In the first lines of his chapter on the BWIR James assumed that the Crown Colony Governments would not interest themselves in publishing a detailed history of the regiment but that such a task would befall a federated West Indies legislature.[2] It is telling for the British Caribbean territories that such an endeavour indeed never came about and that eventually a West Indies Federation was short lived (1958–1962) before each of the colonies went again its own way. As some of his other writings, *The Life of Captain Cipriani* was often reprinted and remained an influential book, not in the least because for decades there was little else on the West Indian experience in the First World War. The subject of James's study, Captain Cipriani, published his wartime memoirs in the early days of the Second World War. To a large extent overlapping with C.L.R. James's political biography, it is of lesser interest to the scholar of the BWIR's presence in Europe as Cipriani was appointed to the 5th Battalion, who throughout the war served in the Middle East. The document, though, gives first-hand information of how a compassionate and sympathetic officer looked upon the management of the BWIR and on the events surrounding the mutiny in Taranto in 1919.

Only in 1982 would the memoirs be published of a man who had belonged to the rank and file of the British West Indies Regiment. Sir Étienne Dupuch, a long-standing newspaper editor and House of Assembly member from The Bahamas, devoted nearly a third of his *A Salute to Friend and Foe* to his service in the British West Indies Regiment, thus proving the importance he attributed to this period of his life. Dupuch was among the first Bahamians to enlist, and he served with the 4th Battalion in Egypt, France, and Belgium. His memoirs added an important perspective on this by then entirely forgotten episode of the war, certainly as little else has been published by BWIR soldiers themselves.

Yet, the publication of Dupuch's memoirs does not mean that no scholarly research had been conducted into the British West Indies Regiment before 1982. By then a whole string of British colonies in the Caribbean Sea had obtained their independence. This triggered scholarly research, and in 1970 and 1971, not long after the declassification of official British records, two contributions had broken the ban of silence on the BWIR. The title of W.F. Elkins' short 1970 essay perfectly covers the content: *A source of Black Nationalism in the Caribbean: The Revolt of the British West Indies Regiment in Taranto, Italy*. And one year later the Guyanese historian Cedric L. Joseph published with his *The British West Indies Regiment 1914–1918* the first historical overview of the regiment. As can be expected from a first study, it was a pretty straight forward descriptive history mainly based on the archives of the Colonial Office and largely focusing on the emergence, the policies, and the organization of the regiment. For more than thirty years it would serve as the only history of the BWIR and can still today be considered an excellent introduction to the subject. Both Elkins and Joseph stressed the connection between the wartime treatment of the West Indian soldiers and the post-war development of anti-colonial movements in the Caribbean. It is an observation that has never been contested and that cannot be denied.

Eye-opening in more than one aspect was the broadcasting in 1999 of the fifty-minute documentary film *Mutiny* produced by Tony T and Rebecca Goldstone of the documentary and heritage interpretation company, Sweet Patootee. The film presented the story of the British West Indies regiment as a tale of 'Black struggle for rehabilitation, pride, and freedom', considering the First World War as 'a defining turning point after the abolition of slavery in the British Caribbean'.[3] Using recently declassified archive material and eyewitness accounts by the few surviving black British First World War veterans, *Mutiny* truly was a pioneering work of public history at a time when as yet not a single academic book had been published on the West Indian involvement in the First World War and only a handful of memoirs or scholarly contributions in journals.

In 2002 Barbadian historian Glenford Howe, whose research had been instrumental in the production of *Mutiny*, published *Race, War and Nationalism: A Social History of West Indians in the First World War* based on his doctoral thesis. Previously some of the book's sections had been published in alternative, earlier forms in Caribbean historical journals. Howe's main question was the impact of the First World War in the West Indies through the participation of its inhabitants in the war and through policy decisions taken in the metropole. Again, Howe puts a particular emphasis on the connection between the different war experiences and the role the veterans played after the war. Howe's work was equally pioneering: due to general ignorance on that episode, some in his homeland considered the black soldiers of the First World War as 'misguided patriots who lacked any sense of race and class consciousness' and thus not worthy to be commemorated.[4] These remarks in the Barbadian press are not unlike those which resounded for many decades in the Republic of Ireland where Irish soldiers of the Great War were often considered collaborators and traitors to the national cause, or those in China downplaying the Chinese Labour Corps as merely ignorant coolies abused in an imperialist struggle.

Two years after the publication of Howe's pioneering study, another doctoral research resulted in *Jamaican Volunteers in the First World War: Race, masculinity, and the development of national consciousness* by British historian Richard Smith. Both Howe's and Smith's books have obvious areas in common, though are also complimentary. While Howe considers the whole of the West Indies, Smith's book is a case study of the Jamaican experience, justifying his choice as an attempt to take sufficient account of territorial distinctiveness.[5] Yet, his book emphasizes something which eminently surpasses territorial confines: the black male body and manhood, as he also explicitly states in the subtitle. If we agree with Smith that skin colour is the most defining factor that makes the Jamaican volunteer different, there is even more reason to compare this experience with that of the other West Indians. One of Smith's points is that besides fear of the impact on Imperial rule and for the image of white superiority, it is primarily a concern for the white masculine identity that explains the British reluctance to deploy non-white troops on the Western Front. I tend to disagree as this is contradicted by the absence of a similar unwillingness in France. Moreover, Richard Smith sometimes goes quite far in explaining phenomena through the prism of the decline of white masculine supremacy, for instance when linking the Somme offensive to the exclusion of black men and white women from the front line in a 'damage-limitation exercise to curtail the erosion of white masculine authority'.[6] For it is precisely after the Battle of the Somme that we see non-white personnel (the Chinese and Indians Labour Corps, the South African Native Labour Corps, the BWIR) arriving *en masse* in Europe, sometimes working very close to the frontline. That they were present in a non-combatant capacity will have done little to enhance the 'white masculine supremacy' in the eyes of locals and the home front.

According to American historian Julian Saltman both Howe and Smith did not sufficiently differ between the BWIR battalions engaged on the Western Front and those deployed in the Middle East. He stresses the fact that unlike their comrades on the Western Front, the battalions in Egypt and Palestine did have combat experience and moreover were not present in Taranto during the revolt which is considered so quintessential by previous scholars. In his 2013 PhD dissertation *"Odds and Sods": Minorities in the British Empire's Campaign in Palestine, 1916–1919,* Saltman not only studied these three BWIR battalions within the broader story of the Egyptian Expeditionary Force, but also compared their treatment and agency with that of three other British 'minority' battalions active within the EEF known as the 'Jewish Legion'. I tend not to agree entirely with his point of departure: while it is indeed important to differentiate between theatres of war, I am not convinced that this is the ultimate and defining factor in war experiences. After all the main context wherein the men lived their experiences was first and foremost that of the British Army whose structure, organization, culture, and ways of thinking were hardly different whether it was fighting in France, in the Balkans, in the Middle East, or elsewhere. Moreover, with only one of the three battalions engaged in battle for a rather brief period, his statement that 'the role of the BWIR battalions in Egypt and Palestine was fundamentally different'[7] is false. Precisely the frustration of not being (more) engaged in a fighting capacity was something both the BWIR men in the Levant and those in Europe, especially those of the 3rd and 4th battalions who had been trained as infantrymen, shared. Likewise, his argument that the EEF battalions were not present in Taranto during the mutiny misses the point that they had been in the same camp experiencing the same racist regime before and after the brief event of the mutiny. And while I appreciate his attempt to compare the war experiences and their impact on two minority groups within the British Empire, his choice of the West Indians on the one hand and the Jews on the other hand, seems rather artificial, and this basically because they were so utterly different: while the Jewish battalions were nearly entirely of white European stock, included many foreign nationals, and were bound together by religion and Zionist aspirations, the West Indian rank and file were black subjects of the British Empire, belonging to different creeds. While political aspirations did play a certain role in their recruitment, it had for the large majority not been the major drive to enlist. By comparing them with an overall white, religious minority that included a large number of foreign nationals, the immensely important, even defining issue of skin colour is downplayed.

In the run-up to, during, and immediately after the centenary of the Great War some initiatives were taken, mainly in the UK, to bring the story of the West Indian involvement in the Great War to a wider audience. Community historian Stephen Bourne published *Black Poppies* in 2014. His book is not based on original research but offers a prism of black British war experiences drawn from other works and aimed at a wider public. Some of its rather short chapters are dedicated to the British West Indies Regiment or to individual men who served therein. A similar approach but more profoundly researched is Barry Renfrew's *Britain's Black Regiments. Fighting for Empire and Equality* from 2020 in which the author gives an overview of the service of black West Indians in the British military, from the late eighteenth century to the aftermath of the Second World War.

Eye-opening in more than one respect was David Olusoga's BBC documentary series and accompanying book *The World's War: Forgotten Soldiers of Empire*. While the series and book had the much wider scope of Indian, African, and Asian troops in the Great War, it made a wide audience aware of the deployment of Caribbean soldiers in the First World War. It is perhaps not a coincidence that shortly later, in July 2017, a memorial dedicated to African and Caribbean soldiers who died in both World Wars was unveiled on Windrush Square in Brixton. Also, in the sphere of 'public history' and with a focus on the West Indians was the exhibition *The Caribbean's Great War*, which was held in the Museum of London Docklands from 6 November 2015 to 2 May 2016. It was organized by – and looked at the subject through the prism of – the West Indian Committee, yet it was the first exhibition dedicated to the West Indian rank and file after a disappointingly small exhibition in the Imperial War Museum *From War to Windrush* in 2008.

Within academia too, attention continued to be paid to the West Indies during the First World War, although we should not exaggerate this either. For Richard Smith, Jamaica and by extension the British Caribbean during World War I remained his main research topic. For example, he collaborated on the important international research project *Cultural Exchange in a Time of Global Conflict: Colonials, Neutrals and Belligerents During the First World War* (CEGC) that ran from 2013 to 2016 and was funded by HERA (Humanities in the European Research Area). As part of this project Anna Maguire wrote a PhD dissertation on the cultural encounters of West Indians, Māori and black South Africans during the First World War. It was published in 2021 as *Contact Zones of the First World War: Cultural Encounters across the British Empire*. Finally, at the moment of writing, John Siblon is completing a PhD at Birkbeck College, London, on how Black colonial servicemen have been represented in the aftermath of the Great War.

So, where are we now? Despite these efforts, the West Indian involvement in the First World War is still pretty much an unknown story, even among scholars of that war. It seems that the uproar caused by the Channel Four documentary *Unremembered – Britain's Forgotten War Heroes*, which aired in November 2019 has set some things in motion. In any case, it forced the Commonwealth War Graves Commission to produce a 'Non-Commemoration Report' and take action. Although the documentary and the CWGC's report primarily relate to Africans (and Asians) in British service who are not (officially) commemorated, it has once again drawn attention to many forgotten groups who fought for King and Country during the wars. And that certainly includes the British West Indies Regiment.

Without claiming to have written the ultimate book on the British West Indies Regiment – something for which much more research would be needed, especially in the former British overseas territories in the Caribbean – my aim with this publication is to contribute to an understanding of what the impact of their First World War experience was on the British Caribbean soldiers and the societies from which they came. I am therefore greatly indebted to people like Tony T and Rebecca Goldstone, Glenford Howe and Richard Smith, who pioneered scholarship into the BWIR with their documentaries and books. At the same time, by a strong focus on the Western Front and on individual experiences, I wanted to approach the subject from a new angle in order to add new insights. I hope that it may be considered a fitting building block and that it will encourage many more to devote themselves to the study of a group of participants in the First World War who have unjustly fallen into the folds of history.

Finally, this book was written for a broad readership. To enhance readability, the number of notes has been greatly reduced: from 310 in the original manuscript to less than 100. The author is always willing to refer scholars to the sources he used.

Acknowledgements

In 2016 I wrote my PhD which eventually was published as *Asia in Flanders Fields. Indians and Chinese on the Western Front, 1914–1920* (Pen & Sword, 2021). Initially, however, I had the intention to include a case study of the British West Indies Regiment in my comparison of non-European troops in British service in France and Flanders. My supervisors Marnix Beyen and Mark Connelly convinced me not to do so and to focus solely on the two Asian groups. The British West Indies Regiment was worth a separate study and publication. It is due to their wise counsel that this book came into being.

The subject first came to my attention in 1999 when during a meal at Julian Putkowski's house in Hackney, I got acquainted with Tony T and Rebecca Goldstone who were then in the final production phase of their ground-breaking documentary *Mutiny*. Some years later, that other pioneer of research on the Caribbean in the First World War, Richard Smith, contacted me to obtain Flemish accounts on the West Indian soldiers for his PhD on the Jamaican volunteers of the Great War. Over the years we would meet regularly at conferences and seminars, such as the ones organized by Paul Cornish and Nicholas Saunders at the Imperial War Museum. Finally, I had the chance to invite Glenford Howe to the 2018 'To End All Wars?' conference organized by my employer, In Flanders Fields Museum in Ypres. I consider it a privilege to have met all protagonists of BWIR scholarship, and to count them among my friends. I consider this book to be a further expansion of the foundations they have laid.

Julian Putkowski and Nicholas Saunders were more than just hosts or conference organizers but have throughout the years provided most valuable feedback.

I had the chance to represent In Flanders Fields Museum as an associate partner in the research project *Cultural Exchange in a Time of Global Conflict: Colonials, Neutrals and Belligerents During the First World War* (CEGC) that ran from 2013 to 2016 and was funded by HERA (Humanities in the European Research Area). I am grateful to Santanu Das, Daniel Steinbach, and Natasha Awais-Dean for including me, as well as to inspirational colleagues and scholars such as Anna Maguire and Suzanne Bardgett with whom I had exchanges on the British West Indies during the project. I am also indebted to Gabriel Christian in Dominica and the USA, Veerle Poupeye and Staci-Marie Dehaney in Jamaica, and Mary Alpuche from the Belize Archives and Record Service. Rachel Manley (Canada) enlightened me on her grandfather and great-uncle Norman and Roy Manley, while Ronald Haynes (USA) was helpful with information on his father Samuel Haynes. Derrian Barrant in Jamaica, Rudi Wille in Belgium, and Mike Reys in London were kind enough to provide me with contemporary pictures of places of West Indian commemoration.

Without the support, interest, and help of my colleagues at In Flanders Fields Museum in Ypres (Belgium) it would have been impossible to realize this book. It is more than justified that a slightly adapted Dutch translation will be published in the museum's series of 'Name List Monographs'. The Name List is the integrated database of all those who died in Belgium (or due to the war circumstances in Belgium) during the First World War, and the monographs focus on often forgotten groups within the war casualties. It entirely ties in with the museum's vision on 'curating war': in an inclusive, and agonistic manner with a focus on individual experiences. All praise to my wife Mieke who again had to put up with me being confined to my desk for days on end, to Georgina Boyes who proofread and edited the English text, to Freddy Rottey who translated the English version into Dutch, to my editor Lester Crook and to publisher Pen & Sword.

* * *

On the islands, as well as in the United Kingdom and on the European continent, individuals and associations continue to commemorate those who came from the Caribbean to give their lives for a freedom and democracy that they themselves were denied. Just one example are my friends from the National Caribbean Monument Charity who are raising funds to erect a memorial at the National Arboretum. Every year, together with inhabitants of Flanders, they lay a wreath at the grave of Herbert Morris, the 17-year-old Jamaican who was executed in Poperinghe on 20 September 1917. It is a small, but symbolically very valuable act that for me touches the essence of what this book, what In Flanders Fields Museum, and what commemorations are about: by commemorating together, we maintain bonds of friendship across borders of nation, culture, and language while we work for a better world and thus ensure that their deaths were not in vain. My deepest gratitude to you, Pauline, Winston, Stephen, Wayne, Gilbert, Paul-Johan, Roos, Theun, Annemie, Pol, Nick, Jim, and everyone else of good will.

Bibliography

Primary Sources
Imperial War Museum, London
Documents 7700: 'Nurse's Autograph Books Containing Contributions by the West Indian Contingent'
LBY EX. 347–350 and S. 6/821: 'West Indian Contingent Committee Reports, 1916–1918'
In Flanders Fields Museum, Ypres (Ieper)
Ms diary of Achiel Van Walleghem
The National Archives, Kew
CAB 23/1: 'Cabinet Office, War Cabinet, Minutes of Meetings, Dec 1916–Feb 1917'
CO 28/292/37: 'Colonial Office, Correspondence, telegram from Secretary of State, 13 October 1917'
CO 318/333: 'Colonial Office, West Indies Original Correspondence, Secretary of State, 1914'
CO 318/336-7: 'Colonial Office, West Indies Original Correspondence, Secretary of State, 1915'
CO 318/341: 'Colonial Office, West Indies Original Correspondence, Secretary of State, April to December 1916'
CO 318/344: 'Report of the West Indian Contingent Committee, 30 September 1917'
CO, 318/348/38: 'Petition from non-commissioned officers of the BWIR requesting equal treatment and pay with British troops'
CO 318/350/2590: 'Colonial Office, Formation of the Caribbean League by members of the British West Indies Regiment. Reports the league's 'seditious nature', 17 December 1918–10 January 1919'
MH 106/2302: 'Medical sheets, 2nd General Hospital, 1917–20'
WO 95/338/1: 'War Diary of the 3rd Battalion British West Indies Regiment, September 1916–June 1919'
WO 95/338/2: 'War Diary of the 8th Battalion British West Indies Regiment, July–December 1917'

WO 95/409/3: 'War Diary of the 4th Battalion British West Indies Regiment, May–November 1918'
WO 95/409/4: 'War Diary of the 7th Battalion British West Indies Regiment, June–December 1917'
WO 95/495/3: 'War Office, War Diary of the 6th Battalion British West Indies Regiment, March 1917–April 1919'
WO 339/111607: 'Service Papers of Major Reginald Elgar Willis'
WO 372/12/9628: 'Medal card Emanuel Latrelle, BWIR, Regt No 12296'
WO 372/3/212359: 'Medal card of Buz Butler, BWIR, Regimental No 793'
WO 372/14/60130: 'Medal card of Henry B. Monteith, BWIR, Regt No 12355'
WO 372/24/92892: 'Medal card of Arthur Laurence McLeod Henry, BWIR, No 1960'
Town Archives Poperinghe
'Register of letters received by the Assistant Provost Marshall, 17 September 1917–8 January 1918'

Secondary Sources
Anon, *Manual of Military Law*, (London: His Majesty's Stationery Office, 1914).
Ashdown P, Marcus Garvey, the UNIA and the Black Cause in British Honduras, 1914–1949. *Journal of Caribbean history*,1981, 15, 41–55.
Aspinal, A, The War Effort of the British West Indies. In: Lucas, CP (ed), *The Empire at War*, vol. II, (Oxford: Oxford University Press, 1923), 325–43.
Bland L, White Women and Men of Colour: Miscegenation Fears in Britain after the Great War. *Gender & History*, April 2005, 17, no. 1, 29–61.
Bolland O N, Labor Protests, Rebellions, and the Rise of Nationalism during Depression and War. In Palmié S and Scarano F A (eds), *The Caribbean. A History of the Region and Its Peoples*, (Chicago: The University of Chicago Press, 2011), 459–74.
——, Butler, Tubal Uriah (1897–1977), Trade Unionist and Politician in Trinidad and Tobago. *Oxford Dictionary of National Biography Online*, n.d.
Bourne S, *Black Poppies: Britain's Black Community and the Great War*, (Stroud: The History Press, 2014).
Brendon P, *The Decline and Fall of the British Empire: 1781–1997*, (London: Vintage, 2008).
Brizan G, *Brave Young Grenadians – Loyal British Subjects: Our People in the First and Second World Wars*, (St George's: author, 2002).
Burns A, *History of the British West Indies*, (London: George Allen & Unwin, 1954).
Buxton H, Imperial Amnesia: Race, Trauma and Indian Troops in the First World War. *Past and Present*, 2018, 241, no. 1, 221–58.

Chamberlain M, *Empire and Nation-Building in the Caribbean. Barbados, 1937–66*, (Manchester: Manchester University Press, 2010).

Chielens P and Trogh P, *De Geschreven Oorlog. Anthologie van Teksten van Het Front in België 1914–1940*, (Antwerpen: Manteau / De Bezige Bij, 2016).

Christian G, *The Interwar Years & the Caribbean Soldier in Social Transformation: A Dominican Perspective.* Pdf, 2010.

Cipriani A A, *Twenty-Five Years after; the British West Indies Regiment in the Great War, 1914–1918*, (Port-of-Spain: Trinidad Pub. Co., 1940).

Costello R, *Black Tommies: British Soldiers of African Descent in the First World War*, (Liverpool: Liverpool University Press, 2015).

Cowley J. Cultural Fusions: Aspects of British West Indian Music in the U. S. A. and Britain. *Popular Music*, 1985, 5, 82–86.

———, London Is the Place: Caribbean Music in the Context of Empire 1900–60. In Oliver, P (ed), *Black Music In Britain: Essays on the Afro Asian Contribution to Popular Music*, (Milton Keynes: Open University Press, 1990), 57–76.

Cundall F, *Jamaica's Part in the Great War, 1914–1918*, (London: Pub. for the Institute of Jamaica by the West India Committee, 1925).

de Lisser H G, *Jamaica and The Great War*, (Kingston: Gleaner Press, 1917).

Dendooven D, The British Dominions and Colonies at the Front in Flanders. In: Dendooven D and Chielens P (eds), *World War I. Five Continents in Flanders*, (Tielt: Lannoo, 2008), 89–115.

———, The United States in Our Region during the First World War. In: Dendooven D and Chielens P (eds), *World War I. Five Continents in Flanders*, (Tielt: Lannoo, 2008), 130–35.

———, *Asia in Flanders Fields. Indians and Chinese on the Western Front, 1914–1920* (Barnsley: Pen & Sword Military, 2021).

Descamps F, Hulptroepen Bij de Britse Legers. Labour Corps. In Vancoillie J, Descamps F, and Vandeweyer L (eds),*Ten Oorlog Met Schop En Houweel: Bijdragen over de Hulptroepen van de Genie van Het Belgische, Duitse En Britse Leger Tijdens de Eerste Wereldoorlog,*(Kuurne: Western Front Association België, 2009), 113–219.

Du Bois C M, Caribbean Migrations and Diasporas. In: Palmié S and Scarano F A (eds), *The Caribbean. A History of the Region and Its Peoples*, (Chicago: The University of Chicago Press, 2011), 583–96.

Duke E D, The Diasporic Dimensions of British Caribbean Federation in the Early Twentieth Century'. *NWIG: New West Indian Guide/Nieuwe West-Indische Gids*, 2009, 83, no. 3–4, 219–48.

———, *Building a Nation: Caribbean Federation in the Black Diaspora.* (Gainesville: University Press of Florida, 2016).

Dupuch E, *A Salute to Friend & Foe*, (Nassau: The Tribune, 1982).

Dyde B. *The Empty Sleeve: The Story of the West India Regiments of the British Army*, (St John's, Antigua: Hansib Caribbean, 1997).
Elkins W F, A Source of Black Nationalism in the Caribbean: The Revolt of the British West Indies Regiment at Taranto, Italy. *Science & Society*, 1970, 34, no. 1, 99–103.
——, Hercules and the Society of Peoples of African Origin. *Caribbean Studies*, 1972, 11, no. 4, 47–59.
Eriksen T H, *Ethnicity and Nationalism. Anthropological Perspectives*, (London: Pluto Press, 1993).
Ewing A, *The Age of Garvey. How a Jamaican Activist Created a Mass Movement and Changed Global Black Politics*, (Princeton: Princeton University Press, 2014).
——, Caribbean Labour Politics in the Age of Garvey, 1918–1938. *Race & Class*, 2013, 55, no. 1, 23–45.
Fraser C, The Twilight of Colonial Rule in the British West Indies: Nationalist Assertion vs Imperial Hubris in the 1930s. *Journal of Caribbean History*, 1996, 30, no. 1 & 2, 1–19.
Fraser P, Some Effects of the First World War on the British West Indies. *Caribbean Societies, Vol. 1. Collected Seminar Papers*, (London: Institute of Commonwealth Studies, 1982).
Geiss I, *The Pan-African Movement*. (London: Methuen, 1974).
Goebel M, Fighting and Working in the Metropole: The Nationalizing Effects of WWI Throughout the French Empire, 1916–1930. In: Bley H (ed), *The World During the First World War*, (Essen: Klartext, 2014), 101–11.
Goldthree R N, "A Greater Enterprise than the Panama Canal": Migrant Labor and Military Recruitment in the World War I-Era Circum-Caribbean. *Labor: Studies in Working-Class History of the Americas*, December 2016, 13, no. 3–4, 57–82.
Grant C, *Negro With a Hat. The Rise and Fall of Marcus Garvey and His Dream of Mother Africa*, (London: Jonathan Cape, 2008).
Hammond M, Blues in the Trenches. John Jacob Niles' Singing Soldiers. In: Das S, Maguire A and Steinbach D (eds), *Colonial Encounters in a Time of Global Conflict, 1914–1918*, (Abingdon: Routledge, 2022), 170–89.
Healy M S, *Empire, Race and War: Black Participation in British Military Efforts During the Twentieth Century*. PhD thesis, (Chicago: Loyola University, 1998).
Healy M S, Colour, Climate and Combat: the Caribbean Regiment in the Second World War. *International History Review*, 2000, 22, no. 1, 65–85.
Higman B W, The British West Indies. In Winks, R (ed),*The Oxford History of the British Empire. Volume V. Historiography*, (Oxford: Oxford University Press, 1999),134–45.

Hill S A, *Who's Who in Jamaica ... A Biennial Biographical Record Containing Careers of Principal Public Men and Women of Jamaica*, (Kingston: Gleaner, 1920).

Horner A E, *From the Island of the Sea: Glimpses of a West Indian Battalion in France*, (Nassau: Guardian Office, 1919).

Howe G D, West Indian Blacks and the Struggle for Participation in the First World War'. *The Journal of Caribbean History*, 1994, 28, no. 1, 27–62.

———, In the Crucible: Race, Power and Military Socialization of West Indian Recruits during the First World War. *Journal of Caribbean Studies*, 1995, 10, no. 3, 163–81.

———, Military-Civilian Intercourse, Prostitution and Venereal Disease among Black West Indian Soldiers during World War I. *Journal of Caribbean History*, 1997, 31, no. 1–2, 88–102.

———, Military Selection and Civilian Health: Recruiting West Indians for World War I. *Caribbean Quarterly*, 1998, 44, 35–49.

———, De(Re) Constructing Identities. World War I and the Growth of Barbadian/West Indian Nationalism. In: Marshall D D and Howe G D (eds), *The Empowering Impulse. The Nationalist Tradition of Barbados*, (Barbados: Canoe Press, 2001),103–32.

———, *Race, War and Nationalism: A Social History of West Indians in the First World War.* (Kingston: Ian Randle Publishers, 2002).

James C L R, *Beyond a Boundary* (London: Hutchinson & Co, 1963).

———,*The Life of Captain Cipriani. An Account of British Government in the West Indies.* (Durham and London: Duke University Press, 2014).

James G, *The Chinese Labour Corps (1916–1920)*, (Hong Kong: Bayview Educational, 2013).

James W, *Holding Aloft the Banner of Ethiopia. Caribbean Radicalism in Early Twentieth-Century America*, (London: Verso, 1998).

Jansen J C and Osterhammel J, *Decolonization. A Short History*, (Princeton & Oxford: Princeton University Press, 2017).

Jenkinson C, *Black 1919: riots, resistance and racism in imperial Britain*, (Liverpool: Liverpool University Press, 2009).

Joseph C L, The British West Indies Regiment 1914–1918. *Journal of Caribbean History*, 1972, 2, 94–124.

Joseph M, First World War Veterans and the State in the French and British Caribbean, 1919–1939. *First World War Studies*, 2019, 10, no. 1, 31–48.

Keene J D, African American Soldiers in a Black World: The Politics of Cultural Interactions. In: Das S, Maguire A and Steinbach D (eds), *Colonial Encounters in a Time of Global Conflict, 1914–1918*, (Abingdon: Routledge, 2022), 217–37.

Killingray D, "A Good West Indian, a Good African, and, in Short, a Good Britisher": Black and British in a Colour-Conscious Empire, 1760–1950. *The Journal of Imperial and Commonwealth History*, 2008, 36, no. 3, 363–81.

———, British Racial Attitudes towards Black People during the Two World Wars, 1914–1945. In: Storm E and Al Tuma A (eds), *Colonial Soldiers in Europe, 1914–1945: 'Aliens in Uniform' in Wartime Societies*, (New York: Routledge, 2016), 97–118.
Lucas C P, *The Empire at War*. 5 vols. (Oxford: Oxford University Press, 1921).
Macpherson A, *From Colony to Nation. Women Activists and the Gendering of Politics in Belize, 1912–1982*, (Lincoln: University of Nebraska Press, 2007).
Maguire A, "I Felt like a Man": West Indian Troops under Fire during the First World War. *Slavery & Abolition*, 2018, 39, no. 3, 602–21.
———, Uncovering the Colonial Cultures and Encounters of the British Empire during the First World War. In: Bessel R and Wierling D (eds), *Inside World War One? The First World War and Its Witnesses*, (Oxford: Oxford University Press, 2018), 207–27.
———, *Contact Zones of the First World War. Cultural Encounters across the British Empire*, (Cambridge: Cambridge University Press, 2021).
———, "A Pageant of Empire?". Untangling Colonial Encounters in Military Camps. In: Das S, Maguire A and Steinbach D (eds), *Colonial Encounters in a Time of Global Conflict, 1914–1918*, (Abingdon: Routledge, 2022), 37–56.
Manley N, The Autobiography of Norman Washington Manley. *Jamaica Journal*, June 1973, 7, no. 1.
Mallet M O, *Letters from the Trenches during the Great War*, (Shipston-on-Stour: King's Stone Press, s.d.)
Martin T, Revolutionary Upheaval in Trinidad, 1919: Views from British and American Sources. *The Journal of Negro History*, 1973, 58, no. 3, 313–326.
McKay C, *A Long Way from Home*, (London: Pluto Press, 1985).
Olusoga D, *The World's War*, (London: Head of Zeus, 2014).
Oram G, *Worthless Men: Race, Eugenics and the Death Penalty in the British Army during the First World War*, (London: Francis Boutle, 1998)
———, *Death Sentences Passed by Military Courts of the British Army, 1914–1924*. (London: Francis Boutle Publishers, 1998).
Putkowski J and Sykes J, *Shot at Dawn: Executions in World War One by Authority of the British Army Act* (London: Leo Cooper, 1999).
Ramson J L, *'Carry on!': Or Pages from the Life of a West Indian Padre in the Field*, (Kingston: Educational Supply Co, 1917).
Renfrew B, *Britain's Black Regiments. Fighting for Empire and Equality*, (Cheltenham: The History Press, 2020).
Rorie D, *A Medico's Luck in the War. Being the Reminiscences of RAMC Work with the 51st (Highland) Division* (Aberdeen: Milne & Hutchison, 1929).
Saltman J T, "Odds and Sods". Minorities in the British Empire's Campaign in Palestine, 1916–1919. Dissertation, University of California, 2013.
Sherlock P M, *Norman Manley* (London: MacMillan, 1980).

Siblon J, Negotiating Hierarchy and Memory: African and Caribbean Troops from Former British Colonies in London's Imperial Spaces. *The London Journal*, 2016, 41, no. 3, 299–312.

Siblon J, 'Race', Rank, and the Politics of Inter-War Commemoration of African and Caribbean Servicemen in Britain. In: Adi H (Ed), *Black British History: New Perspectives*, (London: Zed Books, 2019), 52–70.

Smith R, *Jamaican Volunteers in the First World War: Race, Masculinity and the Development of National Consciousness*, (Manchester and New York: Manchester University Press, 2004).

——, West Indians at War. *Caribbean Studies*, June 2008, 36, no. 1: 224–31.

——, "Heaven Grant You Strength to Fight the Battle for Your Race": Nationalism, Pan-Africanism and the First World War in Jamaican Memory. In: Das S (Ed), *Race, Empire and First World Writing*, (Cambridge/New York: Cambridge University Press, 2011), 265–82.

——, The Black Male Body in the White Imagination during the First World War. In: Cornish P and Saunders NJ (eds), *Bodies in Conflict. Corporeality, Materiality and Transformation*, (London/ New York: Routledge, 2014), 39–52.

——, Loss and Longing: Emotional Responses to West Indian Soldiers during the First World War. *The Round Table. The Commonwealth Journal of International Affairs*, 2014, 103, no. 2, 243–52.

——, World War I and the Permanent West Indian Soldier. In Jarboe A T and Fogarty R S (eds), *Empires in World War I. Shifting Frontiers and Imperial Dynamics in a Global Conflict*, (London: I.B. Tauris, 2014), 303–27.

——, The YMCA and West-Indian Pan-African Encounters during the First World War. The Drury Lane Club for "Coloured Sailors and Soldiers". In: Das S, Maguire A and Steinbach D (eds), *Colonial Encounters in a Time of Global Conflict, 1914–1918*, (Abingdon: Routledge, 2022), 190–213.

——, The Impact of the First World War on the Garvey Movement. In: Hill R (ed), *Marcus Garvey and Universal Negro Improvement Association Papers, XI* (Durham: Duke University Press, n.d.), cclxxv–cclxxxi.

Starling J and Lee I, *No Labour, No Battle: Military Labour during the First World War*, (Stroud: Spellmount, 2009).

Stephens M A, Black Transnationalism and the Politics of National Identity: West Indian Intellectuals in Harlem in the Age of War and Revolution. *American Quarterly*, 1998, 50, no. 3, 592–608.

Tony T and Goldstone R. *Mutiny*. Historical documentary. (London: Sweet Patootee, 1999).

Van Galen Last D, *De Zwarte Schande: Afrikaanse Soldaten in Europa, 1914–1922*, (Amsterdam / Antwerpen: Atlas Contact, 2012).

Van Walleghem A, *Oorlogsdagboeken 1914–1918*, (Tielt: Lannoo, 2014).

Van Walleghem A, *1917. The Passchendaele Year. The British Army in Flanders. The Diary of Achiel Van Walleghem*. (Brighton: EER, 2017).
Wallace E, *The British Caribbean from the Decline of Colonialism to the End of Federation*, (Toronto / Buffalo: University of Toronto Press, 1977).
The West India Committee, *The Caribbean's Great War*, (London, The West India Committee, s.d.)
White N, St William Wellington Grant – A Fighter for Black Dignity. *Jamaica Journal*, 1979, 12–15, no. 43, 56–63.
Winegard T C, *Indigenous Peoples of the British Dominions and the First World War*, (Cambridge: Cambridge University Press, 2012).
Worrell R, Pan-Africanism in Barbados. In Marshall D D and Howe G D (eds), *The Empowering Impulse. The Nationalist Tradition of Barbados*, (Barbados: Canoe Press, 2001), 196–220.
Zumoff J A, Black Caribbean Labor Radicalism in Panama, 1914–1921. *Journal of Social History*, 2013, 47, no. 2, 429–57.

Digital sources
Caribbean Roll of Honour: http://caribbeanrollofhonour-ww1-ww2.yolasite.com/army-ww1.php (last accessed June 2021)
Commonwealth War Graves Commission: http://www.cwgc.org/find-war-dead.aspx (queries performed on 3 October 2016).
Imperial War Museum podcass: thttp://www.iwm.org.uk/history/podcasts/voices-of-the-first-world-war/podcast-25-winter-1916-17 (accessed 2 October 2016).
The Jamaica Observer: http://www.jamaicaobserver.com/columns/Gunner-NW-Manley--MM_18236330 (accessed 3 October 2016).

Notes

Introduction
1. The Crisis, September 1920, Quoted in: Duke, E, The Diasporic Dimensions of British Caribbean Federation in the Early Twentieth Century. *NWIG: New West Indian Guide/Nieuwe West-Indische Gids*, 2009, 83, no. 3–4, p. 241.

Chapter One: The British West Indies
1. Dupuch E, *A Salute to Friend & Foe*, (Nassau: The Tribune, 1982), p. 56.
2. Howe G D, *Race, War and Nationalism: A Social History of West Indians in the First World War.* (Kingston: Ian Randle Publishers, 2002), p. 1.
3. Quoted in Bourne S, *Black Poppies: Britain's Black Community and the Great War*, (Stroud: The History Press, 2014), p. 29.
4. Sherlock P M, *Norman Manley* (London: MacMillan, 1980), p. 24.
5. James C L R, *The Life of Captain Cipriani. An Account of British Government in the West Indies.* (Durham and London: Duke University Press, 2014), p. 52.
6. Eriksen T H, *Ethnicity and Nationalism. Anthropological Perspectives*, (London: Pluto Press, 1993), p. 83.

Chapter Two: A British West Indies Regiment
1. Anon, *Manual of Military Law*, (London: His Majesty's Stationery Office, 1914), p. 471.
2. TNA, CO 318/333: 'Colonial Office, West Indies Original Correspondence, Secretary of State, 1914'.
3. Tony T and Goldstone R. *Mutiny*. Historical documentary. (London: Sweet Patootee, 1999), 09:00–12:00.
4. Du Bois C M, Caribbean Migrations and Diasporas. In: Palmié S and Scarano F A (eds), *The Caribbean. A History of the Region and Its Peoples*, (Chicago: The University of Chicago Press, 2011), p. 584.
5. Tony T and Goldstone R, *Op. Cit.*, 09:00–12:00.
6. Smith R, *Jamaican Volunteers in the First World War: Race, Masculinity and the Development of National Consciousness*, (Manchester and New York: Manchester University Press, 2004), p. 41.

7. Howe G D, *Race, War and Nationalism*, p. 18.
8. Smith R, *Jamaican Volunteers*, p. 48.
9. Quoted in Howe G D, *Race, War and Nationalism*, p. 3; Smith R, *Jamaican Volunteers*, p. 43.
10. Quoted in Tony T and Goldstone R, *Op. Cit.*, 15:00.
11. Quoted in Smith R, The Black Male Body in the White Imagination during the First World War. In: Cornish P and Saunders NJ (eds), *Bodies in Conflict. Corporeality, Materiality and Transformation*, (London/ New York: Routledge, 2014), p. 45.
12. Horner A E, *From the Island of the Sea: Glimpses of a West Indian Battalion in France*, (Nassau: Guardian Office, 1919), p. 63.
13. James C L R, *Beyond a Boundary* (London: Hutchinson & Co, 1963), p. 39–40.
14. Quoted in Tony T and Goldstone R, *Op. Cit.*, 5:45.
15. Howe G D, *Race, War and Nationalism*, p. 37.
16. Tony T and Goldstone R, *Op. Cit.*,15:20.
17. Ibidem, 18:55.
18. Dupuch E, *Op. Cit.*, p. 35–7.
19. James C L R, *The Life of Captain Cipriani*, p. 69.
20. TNA, CO 28/292/37: 'Colonial Office, Correspondence, telegram from Secretary of State, 13 October 1917'; Joseph C L, The British West Indies Regiment 1914–1918. *Journal of Caribbean History*, 1972, 2, p. 104.
21. Mallet M O, *Letters from the Trenches during the Great War*, (Shipston-on-Stour: King's Stone Press, s.d.).
22. IWM, Documents 7700: 'Nurse's Autograph Books Containing Contributions by the West Indian Contingent'.
23. Ibidem
24. IWM, LBY EX. 347-350 and S. 6/821: 'West Indian Contingent Committee Reports, 1916–1918'.
25. TNA, CAB 23/1: 'Cabinet Office, War Cabinet, Minutes of Meetings, Dec 1916 – Feb 1917'.
26. James C L R, *The Life of Captain Cipriani*, p. 71.

Chapter Three: West Indians in France & Flanders
1. TNA, WO 95/409/4: 'War Diary of the 7th Battalion British West Indies Regiment, June – December 1917'.
2. Horner A E, *Op. Cit.*, p. 13–6.
3. Ibidem, p. 32, 39, 44–6.
4. Ibidem, p. 3, 7, 32, 39–40, 49.
5. Dupuch E, *Op. Cit.*, p. 56.
6. Ibidem, p. 78.
7. Quoted in Tony T and Goldstone R, *Op. Cit.*, 22:30; Howe G D, *Race, War and Nationalism*, p. 105.

8. Tony T and Goldstone R, *Op. Cit.*, 21:20.
9. TNA, WO 95/338/1: 'War Diary of the 3rd Battalion British West Indies Regiment, September 1916–June 1919'; TNA, WO 95/338/2: 'War Diary of the 8th Battalion British West Indies Regiment, July–December 1917'; TNA, WO 95/495/3: 'War Office, War Diary of the 6th Battalion British West Indies Regiment, March 1917 – April 1919'.
10. Horner A E, *Op. Cit.*, p. 19.
11. Quoted in Maguire A, "I Felt like a Man": West Indian Troops under Fire during the First World War. *Slavery & Abolition*, 2018, 39, no. 3, p. 612.
12. TNA, MH 106/2302: 'Medical sheets, 2nd General Hospital, 1917–20'.
13. Buxton H, Imperial Amnesia: Race, Trauma and Indian Troops in the First World War. *Past and Present*, 2018, 241, no. 1, p. 243–4.
14. Rorie D, *A Medico's Luck in the War. Being the Reminiscences of RAMC Work with the 51st (Highland) Division* (Aberdeen: Milne & Hutchison, 1929), p. 145.
15. Dupuch E, *Op. Cit.*, p. 58–9.
16. Ibidem, p. 72
17. TNA, WO 95/338/1: 'War Diary of the 3rd Battalion British West Indies Regiment, September 1916–June 1919.
18. Ramson J L, *'Carry on!': Or Pages from the Life of a West Indian Padre in the Field*, (Kingston: Educational Supply Co, 1917), p. 11.
19. Town Archives Poperinghe, Register of letters received by the Assistant Provost Marshall, 17 September 1917–8 January 1918, entries of 3 Nov 1917 and 14 Nov 1917.
20. Horner A E, *Op. Cit.*, p. 4 & 55.
21. Dupuch E, *Op. Cit.*, p. 33–4.
22. In Flanders Fields Museum, ms diary Achiel Van Walleghem; Van Walleghem A, *1917. The Passchendaele Year. The British Army in Flanders. The Diary of Achiel Van Walleghem.* (Brighton: EER, 2017), p. 112–3; Van Walleghem A, *Oorlogsdagboeken 1914–1918*, (Tielt: Lannoo, 2014), p. 110.
23. A photograph, kept in the Bayerische Armee Museum, Ingolstadt, shows what seems like an unknown member of the BWIR in German captivity. The photograph featured on the cover of *Stand To! The Journal of the Western Front Association*, No. 86, August/September 2009.
24. Horner A E, *Op. Cit.*, p. 36.
25. Ibidem, p. 51.
26. Town Archives Poperinghe, Register of letters received by the Assistant Provost Marshall, 17 September 1917–8 January 1918.
27. Dupuch E, *Op. Cit.*, p. 54–5.

Chapter Four: A troublesome demobilisation: mutiny and difficult return

1. Tony T and Goldstone R, *Op. Cit.*, 35:50.
2. Cipriani A A, *Twenty-Five Years after; the British West Indies Regiment in the Great War, 1914–1918*, (Port-of-Spain: Trinidad Pub. Co., 1940), p. 62.
3. Smith R, *Jamaican Volunteers*, p. 133.
4. Joseph C L, The British West Indies Regiment 1914–1918. *Journal of Caribbean History*, 1972, 2, p. 121.
5. Quoted in Howe G D, *Race, War and Nationalism*, p. 154.
6. McKay C, *A Long Way from Home*, (London: Pluto Press, 1985), p. 67–70.
7. Killingray D, British Racial Attitudes towards Black People during the Two World Wars, 1914–1945. In: Storm E and Al Tuma A (eds), *Colonial Soldiers in Europe, 1914–1945: 'Aliens in Uniform' in Wartime Societies*, (New York: Routledge, 2016), p. 101.
8. Tony T and Goldstone R, *Op. Cit.*, 40:00.
9. Smith R, *Jamaican Volunteers*, p. 141.
10. Macpherson A, *From Colony to Nation. Women Activists and the Gendering of Politics in Belize, 1912–1982*, (Lincoln: University of Nebraska Press, 2007), p. 33.
11. Quoted in Zumoff J A, Black Caribbean Labor Radicalism in Panama, 1914–1921. *Journal of Social History*, 2013, 47, no. 2, p. 441.
12. Howe G D, *Race, War and Nationalism*, p. 198.
13. Duke E D, *Building a Nation: Caribbean Federation in the Black Diaspora*. (Gainesville: University Press of Florida, 2016), p. 54.
14. Olusoga D, *The World's War*, (London: Head of Zeus, 2014), p. 401.
15. Aspinal, A, The War Effort of the British West Indies. In: Lucas, CP (ed), *The Empire at War*, vol. II, (Oxford: Oxford University Press, 1923), p. 340.
16. Tony T and Goldstone R, *Op. Cit.*, 44:00.
17. Ibidem, 48:30.
18. Dupuch E, *Op. Cit.*, p. 93.

Chapter Five: Personal trajectories

1. Fraser P, Some Effects of the First World War on the British West Indies. *Caribbean Societies, Vol. 1. Collected Seminar Papers*, (London: Institute of Commonwealth Studies, 1982), p. 1.
2. Chamberlain M, *Empire and Nation-Building in the Caribbean. Barbados, 1937–66*, (Manchester: Manchester University Press, 2010), p. 14 & 41.
3. Quoted in Wallace E, *The British Caribbean from the Decline of Colonialism to the End of Federation*, (Toronto / Buffalo: University of Toronto Press, 1977), p. 29.

4. James C L R, *The Life of Captain Cipriani*, p. 158.
5. Wallace E, *Op. Cit.*, p. 27–8.
6. Wikipedia contributors, Caribbean Regiment, *Wikipedia, The Free Encyclopedia*, https://en.wikipedia.org/w/index.php?title=Caribbean_Regiment&oldid=1102527534 (accessed August 14, 2022).
7. Dupuch E, *Op. Cit.*, p.85, 100–1.
8. James W, *Holding Aloft the Banner of Ethiopia. Caribbean Radicalism in Early Twentieth-Century America*, (London: Verso, 1998), p. 67–9.
9. Manley N, The Autobiography of Norman Washington Manley. *Jamaica Journal*, June 1973, 7, no. 1, p. 7.
10. Personal communication by Rachel Manley, by email on 13 Oct 2020.
11. *The Daily Gleaner*, 27 June 1921, p. 4. Quoted in Smith R, West Indians at War. *Caribbean Studies*, June 2008, 36, no. 1, p. 228.

Chapter Six: West Indian veterans between nationalism and Pan-Africanism

1. Fraser C, The Twilight of Colonial Rule in the British West Indies: Nationalist Assertion vs Imperial Hubris in the 1930s. *Journal of Caribbean History*, 1996, 30, no. 1 & 2, p. 9–10; Bolland O N, Labor Protests, Rebellions, and the Rise of Nationalism during Depression and War. In Palmié S and Scarano F A (eds), *The Caribbean. A History of the Region and Its Peoples*, (Chicago: The University of Chicago Press, 2011), p. 461.
2. Geiss I, *The Pan-African Movement.* (London: Methuen, 1974), p. 5.
3. Worrell R, Pan-Africanism in Barbados. In Marshall D D and Howe G D (eds), *The Empowering Impulse. The Nationalist Tradition of Barbados*, (Barbados: Canoe Press, 2001), p. 198–9.
4. Stephens M A, Black Transnationalism and the Politics of National Identity: West Indian Intellectuals in Harlem in the Age of War and Revolution. *American Quarterly*, 1998, 50, no. 3, p. 592–608.
5. Quoted in Keene J D, African American Soldiers in a Black World: The Politics of Cultural Interactions. In: Das S, Maguire A and Steinbach D (eds), *Colonial Encounters in a Time of Global Conflict, 1914–1918*, (Abingdon: Routledge, 2022), p. 222.
6. James W, *Holding Aloft the Banner of Ethiopia. Caribbean Radicalism in Early Twentieth-Century America*, (London: Verso, 1998), p. 50 & 78.
7. Ewing A, *The Age of Garvey. How a Jamaican Activist Created a Mass Movement and Changed Global Black Politics*, (Princeton: Princeton University Press, 2014), p. 7.

Conclusion

1. Jansen JC and Osterhammel J, *Decolonization. A Short History*, (Princeton & Oxford: Princeton University Press, 2017), p. 42.

2. Smith R, The Impact of the First World War on the Garvey Movement. In: Hill R (ed), *Marcus Garvey and Universal Negro Improvement Association Papers*, *XI* (Durham: Duke University Press, n.d.), p. cclxxix.

Appendix 1: Composition and service of the British West Indies Regiment
1. Based on: TNA, CO 318/344: 'Report of the West Indian Contingent Committee, 30 September 1917'; Aspinal, A, The War Effort of the British West Indies. In: Lucas, CP (ed), *The Empire at War*, vol. II, (Oxford: Oxford University Press, 1923), p. 335; Howe G D, *Race, War and Nationalism*, p. 206.

Appendix 2: Writing the history of the British West Indies Regiment
1. Higman B W, The British West Indies. In Winks, R (ed), *The Oxford History of the British Empire. Volume V. Historiography*, (Oxford: Oxford University Press, 1999), p. 134.
2. James C L R, *The Life of Captain Cipriani*, p. 69.
3. http://www.sweetpatootee.co.uk/work/mutiny/ (accessed 28 September 2016).
4. Howe G D, *Race, War and Nationalism*, p. xv.
5. Smith R, *Jamaican Volunteers*, p. 4.
6. Ibid., p. 79.
7. Saltman J T, "Odds and Sods". Minorities in the British Empire's Campaign in Palestine, 1916 – 1919. Dissertation, University of California, 2013, p. 69.

Index

Adderley, Benjamin, 77
African, The (magazine), 78
Africa, x, xi, 8, 9, 15, 28, 45, 70, 87–89, 104
American Expeditionary Force, 3, 48, 62
Antigua, 1, 5, 6, 8, 95
Anguilla, 1, 6, 95
Aspinall, Sir Algernon, 30
awards;
    Distinguished Conduct Medal, 70
    knighthood, 76
    Meritorous Service Medal, 39
    Military Medal, 44, 79
    National Hero, 14, 79
    Order of the British Empire, 76
    Trinity Cross, 74

Bahamas, xv, 1, 3, 4, 7, 8, 22, 34, 43, 49, 50, 54–56, 63, 70, 75, 76, 80, 82, 84, 92, 95, 97, 98
    Mayaguana, 70
    Nassau, 3, 43, 69, 70, 75, 96
Bahamians, 3, 8, 22, 34, 49, 50, 54, 55, 80, 92, 95, 98
Barbados, xv, 1, 4, 5, 7, 8, 13, 15, 18, 20, 22, 29, 57, 65–67, 71, 72, 84, 86, 90, 95, 99, 100
    Citizens' Contingent, 20
Barbados Herald, The, 71
Barbadians, 65, 99
Barchard, Colonel Arthur Elfinstone, 23, 26
Barnes, James, 70

Battles;
    Battle of the Somme, 100, 101
    Operation Hush, 44
    Third Battle of Ypres, 41, 44, 47, 78, 79
Belgian Army, 39, 40
Belgium, xiv, 29, 31, 32–56, 57, 94, 98
    Abele, 38
    Adinkerke, 40
    Beitem, 37
    Coxyde, 40
    Dadizele, 37
    De Klijte, 53
    Dikkebus, 51
    Elverdinge, 41, 43
    Essex Farm, 33, 39, 46, 48
    Gwalia Farm, 41, 43
    International Corner, 39
    Lendelede, 37
    Loker, 39, 51
    Moorslede, 37
    Nieuport, 40, 44
    Passchendaele, 43
    Poperinghe, 18, 33, 38, 39, 41, 43, 46, 47, 49, 50, 55, 79
    Proven, 36, 37
    Reningelst, 51, 53
    St Sixtus, 39n
    Vlamertinghe, 37, 38
    Watou, 48
    Westvleteren, 39n
    Ypres, xii, 33, 34, 37, 38, 41, 44, 46, 47, 53, 78, 79, 105, 106
    Zwynland, 39
Belize, *see* British Honduras

… Index

Bermuda, ix, 1, 22, 30
Black Nationalism, xvi, 14, 83–90, 93, 98
Bolland, Nigel, 86
Bonar Law, Andrew, 26
Bourne, Stephen, 102
Britain, *see* United Kingdom
British Army;
　XVIII Corps, 46
　Assistant Provost Marshal, 49, 50, 55
　Caribbean Regiment, 87
　Chinese Labour Corps, *see* Chinese
　Duke of Wellington's (West Riding) Regiment, 41
　Egyptian Expeditionary Force, 101, 102
　Egyptian Labour Corps, *see* Egyptians
　Middlesex Regiment, 75
　Officers' Training Corps
　Royal Air Force, 87
　Royal Engineers, 49
　Royal Field Artillery, 78
　West India Regiment, xi, xii, 22, 70
　Wiltshire Regiment, 58
British Empire Workers' and Citizens' Home Rule Party (Trinidad), 74
British Guiana, x, 1, 6, 7, 9, 10, 13, 16, 17, 22, 24, 26, 29, 30, 32, 36, 40, 61, 64, 66, 70, 79, 85, 86, 95
　Georgetown, 6, 10
British Honduras, x, xv, 1, 7, 8, 16–19, 24, 29, 49, 64, 77, 78, 85, 86, 95, 106
　Belize City, 7, 64, 65, 77
British West Indies Regiment;
　1st battalion, xi, 13, 21, 22, 24, 25, 28, 44, 91, 94
　2nd battalion, xi, 21, 22, 24, 25, 91
　3rd battalion, 26, 32, 33, 36–40, 44, 48, 51, 53, 55, 59, 94, 102
　4th battalion, 13, 26, 28, 32–38, 40, 43, 44, 50, 94, 98, 102
　5th battalion, 72, 94, 98
　6th battalion, 18, 29, 36, 38, 44, 46, 48, 58, 94, 96, 97
　7th battalion, 32, 33, 39, 44, 94
　8th battalion, 29, 8, 40, 41, 44, 94
　9th battalion, 18, 23, 32–35, 41, 44, 50, 55, 59, 94, 97
　10th battalion, 3, 37, 44, 59, 94
　11th battalion, 79, 94
　accommodation, xiv, 26, 38, 46
　age, 45
　badge, 27
　casualties, xiv, 29–31, 44–46, 53, 55, 106
　establishment, xi, xiv, 12, 13
　numbers, 28, 29, 94, 95
　officers, xiv, 22, 23, 29, 34–36, 48, 57, 58, 64, 70, 94an
Browne, Gershom, 13, 16
Burden, Herbert, 47
Bustamante, Alexander, 80
Butler, Tubal Uriah 'Buzz', xv, 73, 74, 84
Buxton, Hillary, 41

Caldwell, Major General Sir Charles Edward, 20
Canada, x, 3, 4, 15
　Halifax, 8, 21, 22
Cary–Barnard, Brigadier–General Cyril, 58
Caribs, x, 6, 18, 19, 50
Caribbean League, xv, 59
Cayman Islands, 1, 3, 95
cemeteries
　Adinkerke Churchyard, 40
　Bedford House Cemetery, 41
　Blargies Communal Cemetery Extension, 55
　Boulogne Eastern Cemetery, 38
　Coxyde Military Cemetery, 40
　Etaples Military Cemetery, 45
　Gwalia Cemetery, 43
　La Clytte Military Cemetery, 53
　Mazargues War Cemetery, 45
　Poperinghe New Military Cemetery, 47, 79
　St Sever Cemetery, 45
　Ste Marie Cemetery, 45
　Wimereux Communal Cemetery, 45
Chamberlain, Mary, 71

Chinese, 4, 6, 46–48, 52, 54, 55, 100, 101, 103
Cipriani, Captain Arthur Andrew, xv, 19, 58, 72–74, 83, 97, 98
civilians (Belgian and French), 49–53
Clarion, The (newspaper), 50, 77
Clarke, Eugent, 13, 21, 22, 58, 63, 67, 68
Colonial Office, 7, 12, 15, 23, 24, 26, 60, 63, 72, 75, 85, 99
commemoration, xii, 30–31, 45, 65, 73, 74, 79, 100, 102–104, 106, 107
Commonwealth War Graves Commission, 30, 44, 45, 47, 53, 104
Crisis, The (magazine), 61
Cuba, 2, 67, 89
    Guantanamo, 67
Cundall, Frank, 97

Dacre, Maurice, 41
Dawson, Captain George, 35
de Lisser, Herbert, 19
Democratic League (Barbados), 71
Denham, Edward Dennis, 68
Dominica, 1, 5, 6, 9, 17, 84, 95
Donovan, William Galwey, 15
Du Bois, Christine, 13
Du Bois, W.E.B., ix, 61
Dundonald, Lord, 12
Dupuch, Etienne, xv, 8, 18, 22, 23, 33, 35, 43, 47–50, 54, 55, 63, 69, 70, 75–77, 82, 92, 98

Egypt, xiv, 12, 20, 21, 28, 31, 32, 45, 72, 87, 94, 98, 101
    Alexandria, 22, 28, 55
Egyptians, 46, 47
Elkins, W.F., 98, 99
Empire at War, The (book series), 30, 66, 95, 97
England, *see* Britain
Eriksen, T.H., 10
Ethiopia, 77, 80, 89, 90
execution, 18, 45–47, 97

Federalist and Grenada People, The (newspaper), 15
Ffrench, Leopold, 43–44
Flanders, *see* Belgium
Ford, Arnold, 90
Foreign Enlistment Act (1870), 89
France, xiv, 12, 18, 29, 31–57, 70, 76, 94, 96, 98, 100, 101
    Abancourt, 55
    Armentières, 37
    Bailleul, 37
    Blargies, 55
    Blendecques, 36
    Boulogne, 32, 33, 38, 45
    Brest, 32
    Caestre, 29, 37
    Dunkirk, 47
    Ebblinghem, 36
    Hondeghem, 36
    Marseilles, 32, 41, 45
    Tourcoing, 37
Fraser, Cary, 86
French (language), 5, 6, 9, 32, 35, 50–54
French Army, xi, 4, 14, 34, 35, 52, 53, 92, 103
French Guiana, 53

Garner, Joseph, 72
Garvey, Marcus, xvi, 14, 15, 75, 77, 80, 71, 84, 88, 89
gas, 41
Geiss, Imanuel, 87
George V, King, 9, 13, 20, 39n, 89
Gleaner, The (Daily) (newspaper), 19, 39
Goldstone, Rebecca, 99, 104
Grant, William Wellington, xv, 79–81, 84, 89, 90
Great Britain, *see* United Kingdom
Great Depression, The, 86
Grenada, xv, 1, 5, 8, 10, 15, 16, 18, 22, 29, 48, 57, 60, 65, 70–73, 84, 85, 95
    St George's, 5, 65, 73
Grenadians, 57, 65
Guadeloupe, 6, 53, 54
Guyana, *see* British Guiana

Index 125

Halifax, Lord, *see* Wood, Edward
Harcourt, Lord, 12
Harding, Chester, 66
Harlem Renaissance, 61
Haynes, Samuel, xv, 64, 65, 77, 78, 84, 89, 90, 106
Henry, Lance Corporal Arthur Lawrence McLeod, 39
Hercules, Felix E.M., 62, 84
Higman, Barry W., 96
Horner, Alfred Egbert, 18, 32–35, 38, 50, 54, 96, 97
Howe, Glenford, 9, 99–101, 104
Hutson, Sir Eyre, 64, 65

Independent, The (newspaper), 64
Indian Army, 14, 32, 35, 49, 51, 55, 92, 103
Indians, 4, 6, 14, 24, 55, 76, 92
Imperial War Museum, 24, 103
In Flanders Fields Museum, 105–107
Irwin, baron, *see* Wood, Edward
Italy, xv, 30, 36, 46, 55, 57, 58, 61, 65, 67, 71, 87, 94, 97, 98, 101, 102
Ivor Maxse, General Sir Frederick, 46

Jamaica, xi, xv, 1–4, 8, 10, 11, 13, 14, 16–19, 21–23, 28–29, 34–36, 39, 43–44, 46–48, 51, 55, 57, 59, 61–63, 67–68, 77–80, 84–86, 89–90, 93, 95–97, 100, 103, 105–106
  Kingston, 2, 10, 14, 17, 81
  Westmoreland, 36
Jamaica Standard, The (newspaper), 80
Jamaica Times, The (newspaper), 93
Jamaicans, xi, 3, 14, 17–19, 21–23, 28, 29, 34, 36, 39, 43, 46–48, 55, 57, 59, 61, 67, 68, 79, 80, 96, 100
James, C.L.R., 10, 20, 22, 28, 36, 72, 97
James, Winston, 89
Jews, 101, 102
Joseph, Cedric L., 59, 98, 99
Julien, William Edward, 70

Killingray, David, 62

League of Coloured Peoples, 86
Leeward Islands, 1, 5, 6, 29, 85, 95
literacy, 2, 17, 19, 24, 25, 52, 70, 91
Lucas, Sir Charles Prestwood, 30, 95n, 97

Maguire, Anna, 103
Mallet, Lady Matilda Obarrio, 24
Manley, Norman, xv, 47, 72, 75, 78, 79, 81, 83, 86, 106
Manley, Rachel, 79
Manley, Roy, 47, 75, 78, 79, 106
Manning, Sam, xv, 75
Maroons, 18, 19
Marryshow, T.A., 16, 60, 65, 71, 84
Martinique, 6, 53, 54
McDonald Milliard, Peter, 66
McKay, Claude, 61–62
medical circumstances, 22, 24, 26, 27, 30, 40–45
Mends, Alfred, 85
Mexico, 16
Military Law, 12, 46
Milner, Viscount Alfred, 63
Monteith, Henry B, 93
Montserrat, 1, 5, 6, 95
Moody, Harold, 23n, 86
Morris, Herbert, 18, 41, 45–47
Moyne, Lord, 86
Museum of London Docklands, 103
music, 21, 27, 32–34, 42, 74, 75, 77, 78, 90
Mussolini, Benito, 80, 89
mutiny, xv, 26, 36, 46, 57–60, 65, 67, 97, 98, 102
Mutiny (TV documentary), 13, 34, 67, 99, 105

Negro World (magazine), 61, 71, 88
New Zealand, ix, x, 15, 18, 27, 46, 75, 76, 103
Nimmons, James B., 80

Olusoga, David, 66, 103
Orca (ship), 65

Palestine, xiv, 21, 28, 31, 45, 72, 87, 94, 101
Pan–Africanism, xv, xvi, 14, 61, 75, 78, 83–90, 93
Panama, 2, 3, 13, 24, 25, 66, 95
   Colón, 66
   Panama City, 66
People's National Party (Jamaica), 79
Powell, Clifford, 34, 67
prisoners of war, xiv, 37, 54
Progressive Liberal Party (Bahamas), 76

Ramson, J., 48, 96
Rawle, Cecil, 84
recruitment, xi, 3, 4, 12–14, 16–23, 28–30, 32, 72, 91, 102
Red Summer, 62
religion, 9, 40, 42, 52, 71, 74, 89, 102
Renfrew, Barry, 102
Representative Government Association (Grenada), 84
riots, xv, 10, 11, 17, 19, 36, 62, 63, 65–67, 77, 81, 86
Roach, Norris, 48, 49
Rolle, Emmanuel, 69
Rorie, Major David, 41–43
Royal African Guard, 80
Royal Navy, 3

St Kitts and Nevis, 1, 5, 6, 66, 86, 95
St Lucia, 1, 5, 8–10, 17, 29, 85, 86, 95
St Vincent, 1, 5, 8, 10, 22, 29, 85, 86, 95
Saltman, Julian, 101
Selasie, Emperor Haile, 77
shell shock, 39–41, 47, 48, 68, 69
Sherlock, Sir Philip, 10
Shirley, Ivan, 23
Siblon, John, 103
Smith, Richard, 14, 59, 100, 101, 103, 104
Society of Peoples of African Origin, 62, 84
South African Army, ix, 48, 58, 101, 103
Sparkman, Lance Sergeant Charles S., 43

Stephens, Michelle, 87
strike, 26, 47, 59, 66, 72, 74, 81
Sweet Patootee, 99
Swithenbank, Edna, 79

T, Tony, 99, 104
Taranto, *see* Italy
Tobago, *see* Trinidad and Tobago
trade unions, 8, 72, 74, 81, 85
Tribune, The (Nassau) (newspaper), 76, 96
Trinidad and Tobago, xv, 1, 4, 8, 10, 16–20, 22, 24, 26, 29–30, 59, 62–63, 72–75, 84–86, 95, 97
   Fyzabad, 74
   Planters and Merchants Contingents, 4, 20
   Port of Spain, 4, 10, 19, 63, 73, 74
Trinidad Workingmen's Association, 72, 97
Trinidad Labour Party, 72, 74
Trinidadians, 20, 26, 59, 62, 72, 84, 97
Turks and Caicos Islands, 1, 3, 95

United Fruit Company, 3
United Kingdom, x, xi, xii, xv, 4, 5, 8, 13, 15–17, 26, 30, 45, 62, 65–66, 76, 84, 86, 89, 102
   Brixton, 103
   Deptford, 78
   Dulwich, 23
   London, x, 7, 8, 14, 23, 37, 58, 60–62, 66, 75, 84, 85
   Oxford, 78, 79
   Plymouth, 26, 28
   Richmond, 24
   Seaford, 22, 24, 26–28
   Winchester, 61, 62
   Withnoe, 26
United Negro Improvement Association (UNIA), 14, 15, 61, 72, 73, 75, 77, 80, 88–90
United States of America, xv, 2, 3, 10, 12, 62, 66, 77, 87–90
   Baltimore, 77

Delaware, 77
Florida, 3, 43
Harlem, see New York
Miami, 76, 80
New York, 8, 14, 48, 61, 75, 78, 80, 88, 90
North Carolina, 77
Philadelphia, 77
Pittsburgh, 77
South Carolina, 77

Van Walleghem, Achiel, 51–53
Verdala (ship), 21, 22
veterans' associations, 68, 69, 72, 73, 77, 84, 90
victory parade, 63, 66
Virgin Islands, 1, 5, 6, 95

War Office, 12, 13, 20, 23, 24, 28, 58, 60, 88
weather (impact of), 21, 22, 25, 26, 37, 38

West India Committee, 27, 103
West Indian Contingent Committee, xiv, 26, 27, 30, 37, 57, 60, 67, 74
West Indian, The (newspaper), 16, 48, 65, 72
West Indies Federation, xii, 1, 57, 79, 97
Wickham, Clennell, xv, 13, 71, 72
Willis, Major Reginald Elgar, 35, 36, 58
Windsor, Duke of, 76
Windward Islands, 1, 5
Wood, Edward, 85
Wood–Hill, Lieutenant–Colonel Charles, 28, 81
Workingmen's Association (Barbados), 72
Worrell, Rodney, 87

Yellowlees, Henry, 40
YMCA, 27, 35, 58